GLORY

AS SEEN BY EZEKIEL

GLORY

AS SEEN BY EZEKIEL

Stephen Kaung

Christian Fellowship Publishers, Inc.
New York

Paperback ISBN: 978-1-68062-160-0
eBook ISBN: 978-1-68062-159-4

Available from the Publishers at:

11515 Allecingie Parkway
Richmond, Virginia 23235
www.c-f-p.com

Printed in the United States of America

Preface

Ezekiel was among the captives in the land of Babylon. Humanly speaking, he was in a hopeless situation. His future looked empty and meaningless. And yet, at such an unlikely time, the heavens were opened to Ezekiel, and he saw the glory of the Lord.

In these last days, we, too, find ourselves pressed on every side. How can we survive as Christians? How can we serve God's purpose in our generation?

We believe that God has a way for us, and that way is that we live under an open heaven. Like Ezekiel, we need to catch a glimpse of the glory of the Lord. If we see the glory of the Lord, that will give us light, give us strength, give us direction, and give us purpose. Our life on earth will mean something to the Lord, and it will be fulfillment to us.

We do hope that God will give us a strong desire that we will see His glory. This is one thing that we long for—we want to see the glory of the Lord. If we do, it will give us hope, it will give us faith, and it will give us love that we may press on until the day when the glory of the Lord shall fill the earth as the waters fill the sea.

May the Lord help us. As our brother Kaung prayed before his second message:

Our heavenly Father, how we praise and thank Thee that through our Lord Jesus Christ, Thou hast given us an open heaven. How we praise and thank Thee that Thou hast privileged us with a vision of God, that we may behold the glory of the Lord with unveiled face and be transformed, according to His image from glory to glory, as by the Lord the Spirit. So our Father, as we are all here, we just look up to Thee. We ask that Thy glory shall transform us. We pray that we may hear Thy voice, that we may see Thee and we may see what Thou dost see, that we may be one with Thee. And may we be those who receive grace from Thee. We ask in the name of our Lord Jesus. Amen.

Contents

Note

The author delivered this series of messages in July 1980 before a group of Christians who were gathered together in Richmond, Virginia, for the Christian Family Conference. These recordings were later transcribed for this publication.

Unless otherwise indicated,
Scripture quotations are from the
New Translation by J. N. Darby.

1—The Glory of the Lord Endures Forever

Ezekiel 1:1b—... the heavens were opened, and I saw visions of God.

Ezekiel 1:28bc—This was the appearance of the likeness of the glory of Jehovah. And when I saw, I fell on my face, and I heard a voice of one that spoke.

Psalm 104:31a—The glory of Jehovah will endure for ever

An Open Heaven and Visions of God

Ezekiel 1:1-3—Now it came to pass in the thirtieth year, in the fourth [month], on the fifth of the month, as I was among the captives by the river Chebar, the heavens were opened, and I saw visions of God. On the fifth of the month, (it was the fifth year of king Jehoiachin's captivity,) the word of Jehovah came expressly unto Ezekiel the priest, the son of Buzi, in the land of the Chaldeans by the river Chebar; and the hand of Jehovah was there upon him.

Ezekiel was a captive in the land of Babylon. He was taken captive with King Jehoiachin, and when he was 30 years old, he had already been a captive for five years. We find him "by the river Chebar." The Babylonian Empire had used the captives to dig this Grand Canal, and Ezekiel was found in their midst.

Ezekiel was born into a priestly family, and as we know, one born to a priestly family was to be trained from childhood for the day when he would serve in the holy temple. He was no exception. Before he was taken captive, he was first trained to be a priest. However, when he was 25 years of age—the time a priest would go into the temple as an apprentice—he was taken as a captive. When he was 30 years old—the year that the priest should serve as a full-fledged priest in the temple—he was still in the land of captivity by the River Chebar.

If we think for a little moment, we can realize how painful it must have been for Ezekiel. He was not only a priest by birth but also a priest in heart. There was absolutely no hope of his returning to Jerusalem to serve in the holy temple. On the contrary, Jerusalem would soon be destroyed, and the holy temple would also be completely destroyed. So, humanly speaking, he was in a hopeless situation. There was no hope for his life. His life would become meaningless and empty because his vocation was to serve God as a priest in the temple, but there was no way of ever fulfilling his vocation. His life was indeed empty. But the end of man is the beginning of God.

Here we find in the most unlikely situation, in the most unlikely time, the heavens were opened to Ezekiel, and he saw the visions of God. By that open heaven, that vision of God, Ezekiel saw a new light; it gave him a new meaning. God called him to be a prophet-priest. Even though he was not able to serve in the earthly temple in Jerusalem, yet he was called to serve among the Exiles—the people of God in Babylon—the living temple. He was able to fulfill his life vocation. So, his life was no longer a waste, no longer an emptiness but full and fulfilled. It was all because the heavens were opened to him, and he saw the visions of God.

Now dear brothers and sisters, we who were washed by the precious blood of the Lamb, God has called us to be priests unto God. Our vocation is to serve God. However, we find ourselves in these last days, difficult days, that we are pressed on every side. We find that it is even difficult for us to survive. How can we survive as Christians today? To be a Christian, to live as a Christian, is hard enough. We are struggling every day, trying to live as a believer, as a child of God. But we find that the days are getting more and more difficult. How can we fulfill our vocation as priests unto God? How can we not only survive as believers but also serve God's purpose in our generation in these last days?

Dear brothers and sisters, we believe that God has a way for us. And that way is that we live under an open heaven, that we see the visions of God. Only an open heaven and the vision of God will give us strength and enable us to go through our life, not only just to live, but to live abundantly for the glory of God.

Thank God, an open heaven is our portion today. Why? Because when our Lord Jesus was crucified on the cross, when He shouted, "It is finished," the veil in the temple was rent from top to bottom. The holiest of all was exposed. The way to the holiest of all was opened. So today, by faith, we can enter into the holiest of all, we can live under an open heaven, and we can live to see the glory of the Lord with unveiled face. This is our portion.

What is an Open Heaven?

Ezekiel 1:1b—the heavens were opened, and I saw visions of God.

Now brothers and sisters, what is an open heaven? What does it mean that we live under an open heaven? Of course, an open heaven means so much. It is all-inclusive. We may say that all things that pertain to spiritual life are included in that open heaven.

Communication

An open heaven means, first of all, that there is communication. There is communication between the earth and heaven. There is fellowship, communion, between man and God. It is our portion, our daily portion, that our Lord Jesus has obtained for us. We, as His children, could and should live daily in uninterrupted communion and fellowship with the God of heaven.

The Presence of the Lord

An open heaven means the presence of the Lord with us. Not only will there be communication, but the Lord himself is present with us. The Lord of heaven is with us. We can live in the abiding presence of the Lord.

Knowing the Will of Heaven

An open heaven means that we may know the will of heaven. Heaven will reveal God's mind to us. By the open heaven, we may know what His will is, what His purpose is.

Receiving Strength from Heaven

An open heaven means that we may receive strength from heaven. We may not only know the will of God, but we will be given the power to do the will of God.

A Heavenly Position

An open heaven means that we are given a new position. Though we live on earth, our position today is heavenly. We are seated with Christ in the heavenlies. This is our position. And because of this position, it gives us the ground—the victory—over Satan, over all the evil forces, and everything that is in this world.

Our Portion

Dear brothers and sisters, an open heaven is our portion. Let us take it by faith, thanking the Lord that heaven is open to us. Let us thank the Lord that since heaven is open, we shall be given the spirit of wisdom and revelation.

The greatest need among God's people today is this matter of vision and revelation. In other words, God's people today seem not unable to see what God wants us to see nor hear what God wants us to hear. God's people seem to lack the knowledge of God's perfect will. God's people seem to be ignorant of the eternal purpose of God. It is all because we do not have vision. But remember that vision is our portion because heaven is open to us. And if heaven is open to us, we *cannot but see vision*. We *cannot but receive revelation*.

What Did Ezekiel See?

The heavens were opened, and Ezekiel said, "I saw visions of God." What did he see? He saw a cloud, a bright cloud, coming from the north. And then, as it came closer to him, he saw in that bright cloud four living creatures. And beside the four living creatures he saw the wheels—wheels within wheels. And then he saw above the heads of the living creatures an expanse like terrible crystal, a transparent sea. And then above the sea, he saw a throne, and upon the throne, the likeness of the glory of the Lord.

In the vision that Ezekiel saw, the very center of that vision was God. Whenever heaven is open to you, you will see God because God is the center of everything.

You know, brothers and sisters, our problem today is as if heaven is closed to us and all we see is the earth and the things that are around us. We see things, we see people, we see our circumstances, we see all the things around us, and this is why our life is a struggle. We find that for us to survive is difficult. We find that we are not able to breathe. We are not able to serve God as we should. We have lost sight of God. What we need today is to see God. If heaven is opened to us, we will see Him high and lifted up. In the Scripture, whenever heaven is open, people invariably see God upon the throne.

Ezekiel saw the appearance of the likeness of the glory of the Lord. Why does he use such an expression: "the appearance of the likeness of the glory of Jehovah" (1:28)? It is because no one can see God. God is invisible, but what man can see is the glory of God. What man can see is the likeness of the glory of God. What man can see is the appearance of the likeness of the glory of God.

Now, by seeing the appearance of the likeness of the glory of God, you see God. You see the reality there; you get the impression there. You know, brothers and sisters, what is described in the first chapter of Ezekiel in the vision of God is actually an impression. It is not something just physical. You have to use some physical terms to describe it—like fire, brightness, and glowing brass. These are just descriptive words, trying to give you an impression. And through that impression, you may get the reality of who God is and what God is like. So, what Ezekiel saw was the glory of the Lord.

What is the glory of the Lord? In the Scripture, the most difficult term to define is *glory*. Of course, the Bible never defines anything because once you define something, you confine it. And with God, He is infinite. Therefore, you find in the Scripture, it never defines anything. For instance, when we talk about righteousness, we say righteousness is an act of God. Whenever God does something, it must be right. What is holiness? We can even say holiness is the nature of God because God is holy. He is different. He is unique. He is not common. He is not like us. He stands alone. He is *holy*.

But when we come to this matter of glory, we find it is very difficult to describe. And yet in the Scripture, we find the glory of the Lord, the Lord of glory appeared, and all we can see of God is glory. We cannot see God himself. All we can see is the glory of the Lord. When the glory of the Lord shall appear, we meet God, see Him, and find Him in the glory.

What is Glory?

I remember our dear brother Watchman Nee said, "Glory is God appearing." Now, that is evident because in the Bible, whenever God appears, you see glory. If

God does not appear, it is darkness, it is shame, it is dead. But whenever God appears, there is glory.

When Abraham was in Ur of Chaldea, he was no different from the other people in the world. He lived in a city of idols. We are told by tradition that his father was an idol maker. And probably, Abraham was brought up as an idol worshiper too. But the Scripture says, "One day, the Lord of glory appeared to Abraham" (see Acts 7:2). And when the Lord of glory appeared to Abraham, it changed his life. Abraham was called out of his kindred, out of his land, to follow God to the land that God promised to him. Abraham became a pilgrim and a stranger upon the earth. And from that day onward, he was looking forward to the city with "foundations, whose builder and maker is God" (see Hebrews 11:10). The Lord of glory appeared to him and that changed his life's course.

Dear brothers and sisters, is it not true? Whenever God appears, you cannot remain the same. Sometimes people say, "Stephen, you haven't changed much. You look like you did last year." Now, this may be a compliment in one sense, but in another, I should feel really bad about it because I *should* have changed. If I have seen the Lord, if the Lord has appeared to me, I could not be the same as I was last year. If God's appearing to Abraham changed him, surely His appearing to us will not leave us the same. We have to go on with Him. We have to change and be transformed from glory to glory according to His image by the Lord the Spirit (see II Corinthians 3:18). If God shall appear to us, there is bound to be something happening in us. Oh, how we need to see the glory of the Lord!

Brothers and sisters, we may listen to messages, we may read the Scripture ourselves, we may seem to be very zealous and earnest for the Lord, but all these are external. Unless the glory of the Lord should appear to us, all these will not change us very much. What we need is to see the glory of the Lord.

That was the very burden of Moses. Moses said, "Show me Thy glory. That is all I want" (see Exodus 33:18). We want to see the glory of the Lord. If only the Lord would appear to us, that is glory. And that glory will transform us and conform us to His image.

But what is glory? I remember dear brother T. Austin-Sparks said, "Glory is when God is satisfied. Whenever God is satisfied, you see glory." And that is true because after Moses finished building the tabernacle according to the pattern on the Mount, then you find the glory of the Lord appeared and filled the tabernacle. Why? Because God was satisfied. He was happy.

The same thing was true with the temple that Solomon built. Solomon built the temple according to the pattern that God gave to his father, David. He was the wisest of men, building everything according to the heavenly pattern. Because it was done according to God's pattern, once completed, fire came down from heaven and burned the burnt offering, and the glory of the Lord filled the temple, and the priests had to retreat. God was fully satisfied.

In the life of our Lord Jesus, we behold the glory, as the glory of the only begotten of the Father (see John 1:14). Why? Because in Him, God is always satisfied. God finds His rest in Him. God is happy. God is pleased.

Dear brothers and sisters that is what glory is. Whenever God is satisfied with us, both as individuals and as a corporate body, we will see the glory of the Lord. Oh, what a shame if we should walk through this life and the glory of the Lord is not manifested in us! What a failure it must be if we as a company of God's people are worshiping the Lord together, serving the Lord together, and yet the glory of the Lord is not in our midst! And when people come into our midst, if they cannot sense the presence of the Lord, if they cannot bow down and say, "The Lord is indeed in your midst," then everything is just superficial, empty, and meaningless.

What Are We Seeking For?

What is it that we really desire above all things? It is not spirituality. It is not success. What we *really* seek is the glory of the Lord. If we have the glory of the Lord, then that is everything. If we do not have the glory of the Lord, brothers and sisters, we have nothing ... just nothing. How important it is that we have the glory of the Lord, that the Lord be satisfied! That is our reward. Unless God is satisfied, how can we be contented?

How sad it is that many of God's people today are contented. They seem to be happy with what they think they have and even boast of it. And yet the glory of the Lord is not there. How easily we are contented. Oh, that the Lord would stir our hearts that we will not rest! We will press on! We will seek the glory of the Lord above all things!

A Bright Cloud of Glory

Ezekiel 1:4—And I looked, and behold, a stormy wind came out of the north, a great cloud, and a fire infolding itself, and a brightness was about it, and out of the midst thereof as the look of glowing brass, out of the midst of the fire.

In that vision, Ezekiel saw a cloud coming from the north. According to Isaiah 14:13, it seems as if God's throne is set in the north, in the recesses of the north. So here you will find a cloud coming from the north and it was a bright cloud.

Psalm 18:10-12 says:

And he rode upon a cherub and did fly; yea, he flew fast upon the wings of the wind. He made darkness his secret place, his tent round about him: darkness of waters, thick clouds of the skies. From the brightness before him his thick clouds passed forth: hail and coals of fire.

God rode upon the cherub, flying. He flew fast upon the wings of the wind. Now, outside there might be a dark cloud, but within the dark cloud, there would be brightness. In other words, here you find the brightness of the cloud, and God was riding upon that cloud.

We wonder if this is the same cloud that appeared to the three disciples when they were with Christ on the Mount of Transfiguration. Our Lord Jesus took the three disciples to the Mount of Transfiguration. And when Peter said, "Lord, ... let us make here three tabernacles," suddenly Moses and Elijah disappeared, and a bright cloud covered them (see Matthew 17:1-5a). We wonder if this was the same cloud and the *shekinah* glory of God came in and covered them.

The Four Living Creatures

Ezekiel 1:5-11—Also out of the midst thereof, the likeness of four living creatures. And this was their appearance: they had the likeness of a man. And every one had four faces, and every one of them had four wings. And their feet were straight feet; and the sole of their feet was like the sole of a calf's foot; and they sparkled as the look of burnished brass. And they had the hands of a man under their wings on their four sides; and they four had their faces and their wings: their wings were joined one to another; they turned not when they went; they went every one straight forward. And the likeness of their faces was the face of a man; and they four had the face of a lion on the right side; and they four had the face of an ox on the left side; they four had also the face of an eagle. And their faces and their wings were parted above; two [wings] of every one were joined one to another, and two covered their bodies.

As the cloud came a little closer, Ezekiel saw four living creatures. These four living creatures are a mystery. Now, I do not pretend to know what that mystery is, but it is fascinating. There were four living creatures in that cloud. These four living creatures were cherubim. How do we know they are cherubim? Because in Ezekiel 10:15, it says that these four living creatures are the cherubim. (Cherub is the singular number, and cherubim the plural number.)

Who Are the Cherubim?

The first mention of cherubim is found in Genesis 3:24. After Adam and Eve sinned against God, they were driven out of the Garden of Eden. And God set up cherubim with the flame of flashing sword to guard the way to the Tree of Life. That was the first mention of cherubim, but there was no description.

Then when Moses was in the wilderness, God commanded him to build the tabernacle. And in the tabernacle was the ark, and above the ark, the mercy seat, which is the throne of God. And in making the mercy seat, God commanded Moses to make two cherubim with their wings spread to cover the ark, and their faces were towards the ark. And not only that but on the veil that separates the holiest from the holy place, there were cherubim embroidered all over that veil. Even on the ten curtains that formed the tabernacle, you find cherubim embroidered there.

Now strange to say, Moses had no trouble making these cherubim, even though there was no description. It seems as if they knew then who or what these cherubim were like. All we know is these cherubim have wings and faces, but we do not know what kind of faces. However, Moses had no problem. He made these cherubim; he embroidered these cherubim in the tabernacle.

After that, of course, at the time of Solomon, when Solomon built the temple, he used olive wood and built two gigantic cherubim ten cubits high. And these two cherubim, when they spread their wings, they covered the whole length of the holiest of all. These two olive wood cherubim formed a kind of setting for the ark and the mercy seat (see I Kings 6:23).

So, in the holiest of all, there were four living creatures—four cherubim—two on the mercy seat and two standing behind. And on the folding door, on the wall, there were cherubim all over, and even in the base of the laver, on the panel, cherubim were carved there. There was no description of them, yet Solomon had no problem making them.

It is not until the book of Ezekiel that the living creatures are described. Only two books in the Bible describe these living creatures—these cherubim. One is in the Old Testament—Ezekiel; the other is in the New Testament—Revelation. Only in these two books will you find these living creatures, or cherubim, described. But even though they were described, you will find these cherubim change their form from time to time. Sometimes they have six wings, sometimes they have four wings. They do not seem to remain always the same; they are so flexible, volatile.

Now who are they? Sometimes the Bible says these cherubim are angelic beings, and they are. But sometimes the Bible says they have the appearance of a man, and they do. So, who are they?

Brothers and sisters, may I offer an explanation? You may take it or leave it. I believe these cherubim, or living creatures, are the composite of spiritual realities concerning God's creation. These cherubim represent spiritual principles. But remember, these are not abstract. Sometimes we think that spiritual principles are just abstract ideals. No. These spiritual principles are realities. And the realities are more real than physical things. These cherubim represent spiritual principles and realities of creation in God's mind.

When Moses built the ark and the mercy seat, he built everything according to the heavenly pattern shown to him on the Mount. In other words, whatever Moses and Solomon built on earth was just a representation, just a shadow of the reality that is in heaven. So, the cherubim that cover the ark are a shadow, a reflection, of what is there in heaven at the throne of God. Therefore, in Ezekiel 28, when it mentions that God created the angelic being we now call Satan, he was an anointed, covering cherub. In other words, he was one of the cherubim that were to cover the throne of God.

So, first of all, the cherubim are angelic beings because in God's creation, they are the highest of His creation. Therefore, the cherubim at that time are angelic beings. They represent the idea, they represent the will, they represent the purpose or full thought of God concerning creation.

Then as Adam and Eve were driven out of the Garden of Eden, the cherubim appeared. Why? Why did the cherubim appear at that moment? Because it served as a kind of contrast. Man was created in God's image. Man was to reflect the glory of the Lord. But man had sinned, man had failed, man had not fulfilled his mission.

Though man had failed, God's purpose concerning man remained the same. So, the cherubim stood there as a contrast to the fallen man. Even though man had fallen, God's purpose concerning His creation, and especially man, remained the same. God will yet get what He had ordained for His creation. So that is why you will find cherubim there had the face of man.

God chose the children of Israel as His chosen people. That nation was God's chosen people. Out of all nations, God chose them. They were to be that vessel to stand with God, guarding, as it were, the rights of God and executing God's will. They were a nation to represent God and to manifest God's glory. That is why we find these cherubim all around in the tabernacle and in the temple. We may say that the nation of Israel was God's cherubim under the old covenant, but they failed.

Who Are God's Cherubim Today?

Who are God's cherubim today? The church of God is to be God's cherubim today. These cherubim represent God's thought about the church. We are supposed to be God's vessel, God's instrument. We are supposed to be those that guard and keep the testimony of Jesus. We are supposed to be those that do the will of God, to bring the will of God upon the earth as it is in heaven. So actually, the cherubim of God today are the church of God. One day the cherubim disappeared. In the holy city, the New Jerusalem, there is no cherub nor cherubim. Why? Because God's purpose concerning His creation is fully fulfilled.

God's Creation

Why do we say that these cherubim represent God's creation? You find these cherubim have four faces, the face of a man because man is the king of the earth, then the face of an ox, the king of domestic animals, then the face of a lion, the king of beasts, and the face of an eagle, the king of the birds of the air. So, they represent God's creation. They are four in number because four is the number of creation, of the universality of creation.

Spiritual Discernment

These living creatures are most intelligent. In the book of Revelation, we find they are full of eyes; all the living creatures are full of eyes. And then, in Ezekiel, we will find the eyes on the wheel. And the rim was high and terrible and full of eyes. Why? It speaks of spiritual discernment. These living creatures are full of intelligence, are full of knowledge, are full of spiritual discernment. And because they are full of spiritual discernment, they cry day and night, unceasingly, "Holy, holy, holy, Lord God Almighty who was and who is and who is to come" (4:8b). That is their knowledge. They know God. They know God is holy, unique, different, separated, above all things, alone, almighty, and eternal. He never changes. He always remains the same. And these living creatures—these cherubim—were connected with the holiness of God.

In other words, these cherubim know God. They were so intelligent. They were there always praising and worshiping God and leading the whole creation into worship.

Is it not true that the church today is to lead all creation in worship? Is it not true that we are supposed to be intelligent enough to know God, and in knowing Him to worship Him, and to bring the whole creation to His feet?

God's Will

Ezekiel 1:12-20—And they went every one straight forward: whither the Spirit was to go, they went; they turned not when they went.

And as for the likeness of the living creatures, their appearance was like burning coals of fire, as the appearance of torches: it went up and down among the living creatures; and the fire was bright; and out of the fire went forth lightning. And the living creatures ran and returned as the appearance of a flash of lightning.

And I looked at the living creatures, and behold, one wheel upon the earth beside the living creatures, toward their four faces. The appearance of the wheels and their work was as the look of a chrysolite; and they four had one likeness; and their appearance and their work was as it were a wheel in the middle of a wheel. When they went, they went upon their four sides; they turned not when they went. As for their rims, they were high and dreadful; and they four had their rims full of eyes round about. And when the living creatures went, the wheels went beside them; and when the living creatures were lifted up from the earth, the wheels were lifted up. Whithersoever the Spirit was to go, they went, thither would [their] spirit go; and the wheels were lifted up along with them: for the spirit of the living creature was in the wheels. When those went, they went; and when those stood, they stood; and when those were lifted up from the earth, the wheels were lifted up along with them: for the spirit of the living creature was in the wheels.

And there was the likeness of an expanse over the heads of the living creature, as the look of the terrible crystal, stretched forth over their heads above. And under the expanse were their wings straight, the one toward the other: every one had two which covered on this side, and every one had two which covered on that side their bodies. And when they went, I heard the noise of their wings, like the noise of great waters, as the voice of the Almighty, a tumultuous noise, as the noise of a host: when they stood, they let down their wings; and there was a voice from above the expanse that was over their heads. When they stood, they let down their wings.

The cherubim of God, these living creatures, move swiftly. They are like lightning. And they always go straight; they never turn back or turn around. Wherever they go, they go straight. They go straight to the north, the south, the east, and the west because they have four faces. And the wheels are wheels within wheels, so they do not need to turn. It is always straight. And they are swift in going.

Brothers and sisters, what is above them? The expanse, the throne of God. In other words, they are not only highly intelligent, but they are swift in doing the will of God. They are the chariot of the throne of God. They carry the throne of God everywhere He desires to go. And they are swift in executing the will of God. Their spirit is in the wheel. Wherever the Spirit of God moves, they move. The wheel moves because the spirit of the living creatures is in the wheels, and the spirit of the living creatures is one with the Spirit of God.

Oh, dear brothers and sisters, you will find no distance from God's will. There is not a split second of delay. They move as the Spirit moves because their spirit is one with the Spirit of God. Is that not a description of what the church is in God's mind?

There are many things we can say, but suffice it to say that these living creatures, on the one hand, guard the throne of God; on the other hand, they carry the throne of God. What is the church of God in the mind of God? The church of God is that corporate vessel that keeps the testimony of Jesus and guards it. The church of God is that vessel. It is the chariot of the throne of God. We are to carry, execute, and do the will of God. We are to bring the will of heaven upon this earth through the church—"Thy will be done on earth as it is in heaven."

But brothers and sisters, the church is just a vessel of God. Do not end with a vision of the church. The church is just a chariot—however attractive, beautiful, useful, effective, and wonderful it may be—it is for the throne of God. It is for God alone.

God's Traveling Throne

Ezekiel 1:26-28—And above the expanse that was over their heads was the likeness of a throne, as the appearance of a sapphire stone; and upon the likeness of the throne was a likeness as the appearance of a man above upon it. And I saw as the look of glowing brass, as the appearance of fire, within it round about; from the appearance of his loins and upward, and from the appearance of his loins and downward, I saw as it were the appearance of fire, and it had brightness round about. As the appearance of the bow that is in the cloud in the day of rain, so was the appearance of the brightness round about.

This was the appearance of the likeness of the glory of Jehovah. And when I saw, I fell on my face, and I heard a voice of one that spoke.

Let us notice one thing about the throne of God. Here it mentions how above the expanse, which is above the cherubim, is a likeness of a throne, and the throne has the appearance of a sapphire stone. If you read the book of Revelation, chapter four, you find the throne of God that John saw in heaven was like a stone of jasper and a sardius, but here in Ezekiel, the throne looks like a sapphire stone. It is blue. Why is this stone different from the one in Revelation 4? Some people suggest that God actually has two thrones. Does that shock you? God has a permanent throne set in heaven and a traveling throne.

In the book of Job, Satan appeared before the throne of God (see 1:6). You wonder: If Satan was already cast out of heaven, why was he allowed to go to heaven and appear before the throne of God? I personally believe that Satan did not appear before that permanent throne of God. He appeared before the traveling throne of God.

God travels on the wings of the wind. He travels on the chariot of the cherubim. He travels to look after His creation. He travels all around to see what is happening. Our God is very active. Our God is very interested in His creation. Our God is most concerned with His creation and knows everything that is going on. This is why He has a traveling throne. And it is to that traveling throne that Satan appeared. What Ezekiel saw was not the permanent throne of God in heaven. He saw that traveling throne of God.

So far as Ezekiel was concerned, he would have felt that he was at the end of his life. He was 30 years old and was to be a priest in the temple, but there was no hope for that. To him, it was not only the end of his life, it was the end of the world. To him, everything was lost, everything was finished. He must have been in deep distress, despair, disappointment. There was no hope. Everything was dark, bleak, and black. Was God dead? No! There, Ezekiel saw the throne of God. There, he saw God was traveling. There, he saw God was interested in and concerned with His people. God had not forsaken His people. There, he saw that God was still on the throne. And not only was God on the throne, but the cherubim were there. In other words, all of God's thoughts concerning His people remained the same.

> "Change and decay in all around I see;
> O Thou who changest not, abide with me."[1]

Brothers and sisters, you may find everything on earth has changed. And we do see everything changing.

---

[1] From the hymn, "Abide with Me" by Henry F. Lyte.

There is nothing firm to stand on. Everything is decaying. Everything is now corrupted. We find everything is bleak, black, and hopeless. You may be in despair and disappointment, but dear brothers and sisters, remember this one thing: God is still on the throne. Remember that the throne is carried by the cherubim. Remember that whatever God has ordained for us, whatever God has ordained for His church, whatever God has ordained for the nation of Israel, whatever God has ordained for the whole creation remains unchanged in the sight of God. It is always there, and it will be there forever. How we thank God.

Brothers and sisters, if only we have vision of God, if we only look up and see God on the throne, we will see that He is in charge! He *is*! He knows. He is watching. He is working. He is active. He is ruling and overruling. He is bringing everything upon this earth, in accordance with that vision Ezekiel saw, according to the cherubim that Ezekiel saw. Everything God has ordained for His people, for the whole creation, will eventually be brought to the satisfaction of God.

Psalm 104:31 says, "The glory of Jehovah will endure forever." In other words, the glory of the Lord never changes. We may not see His glory, and yet the glory of the Lord endures forever. It is always there, and in the presence of God, His will is already finished. His purpose is already fulfilled. The church is already there. The holy city, the New Jerusalem, is complete there. It is always there.

"The glory of the Lord endureth forever." "Blessed be the glory of Jehovah from *his* place!" (Ezekiel 3:12). What we need to do is to catch a glimpse of that glory and that will give us hope. That will give us faith. That will give us love that we may press on until that day when the glory of the Lord shall fill the earth, as waters fill the sea. May the Lord help us.

Our heavenly Father, how we praise and thank Thee that the glory of the Lord endures forever. We do praise and thank Thee. Things may change upon this earth—we may change, everything may change—but the glory of the Lord endures forever. Oh, how we praise and thank Thee that Thou art satisfied with what Thou hast purposed. Thou hast already obtained in Thy Son what Thou hast ordained. We only pray that our eyes may be opened, that we may be strengthened by the glory of the Lord to press on unto that fullness that Thou hast ordained for Thy church, and for the whole creation, that Christ may be glorified in the church. In the name of our Lord Jesus. Amen.

2—The Glory of the Lord Departed

Ezekiel 8:1-6—And it came to pass in the sixth year, in the sixth [month], on the fifth of the month, that [as] I sat in my house, and the elders of Judah sat before me, the hand of the Lord Jehovah fell there upon [me].

And I looked, and behold, a likeness as the appearance of fire; from the appearance of his loins and downward, fire; and from his loins and upward, as the appearance of brightness, as the look of glowing brass. And he stretched forth the form of a hand, and took me by a lock of my head; and the Spirit lifted me up between the earth and the heavens, and brought me in the visions of God to Jerusalem, to the entry of the inner gate that looketh toward the north, where was the seat of the image of jealousy, which provoketh to jealousy. And behold, the glory of the God of Israel was there, according to the appearance that I saw in the valley.

And he said unto me, Son of man, lift up now thine eyes toward the north. And I lifted up mine eyes toward the north, and behold, northward of the gate of the altar, this image of jealousy in the entry. And he said unto me, Son of man, seest thou what they do? the great abominations that the house of

Israel commit here, to cause me to go far off from my sanctuary? And yet again, thou shalt see great abominations.

Ezekiel 11:22-25—And the cherubim lifted up their wings, and the wheels were beside them; and the glory of the God of Israel was over them above. And the glory of Jehovah went up from the midst of the city, and stood upon the mountain which is on the east side of the city. And the Spirit lifted me up, and brought me in the vision by the Spirit of God into Chaldea, to them of the captivity; and the vision that I had seen went up from me. And I spoke unto them of the captivity all the things that Jehovah had shewn me.

A year passed since the heavens were opened to the prophet Ezekiel by the River Chebar when he realized that the glory of the Lord endures forever. That vision delivered him out of despair and into hope. That delivered him out of emptiness and purposelessness into usefulness and meaningfulness. God made him a prophet-priest. He was able to serve the purpose of God among the captives. His life became meaningful and effective. And it is all because the glory of the Lord appeared to him.

Seeing His Glory

Ezekiel 1:28bc—This was the appearance of the likeness of the glory of Jehovah. And when I saw, I fell on my face, and I heard a voice of one that spoke.

When the glory of the Lord appears to us, it is our salvation. What we need today, above all things, is to live under an open heaven and see the vision of God. What we need today is to see the glory of the Lord. If we see the glory of the Lord, all our problems are solved. It will give us light, strength, direction, purpose, and ministry so that our life on earth will mean something to the Lord. And, of course, it will be a fulfillment to us as well. So, we do hope that God will give us a strong desire to see His glory. This is one thing we long for—we want to see the glory of the Lord.

The glory of the Lord endures forever. All things have changed and are changing all around, and we may even change, but the glory of the Lord endures forever. There you will find the throne of God. There you will find Him who sits upon the throne. There you will find the cherubim that carry the throne wherever God wants to go. In other words, the purpose of God concerning man, the purpose of God concerning the whole creation, remains forever before God. It is there, and one day we will be there.

So brothers and sisters, what we need is to catch a glimpse of that glory. And that glory will deliver us from despair, disappointment, and frustration. It will lift us up into the very purpose of God. And our life will live in His will.

Called as a Prophet

> Ezekiel 2:3-5—And he said unto me, Son of man, I send thee to the children of Israel, to nations that are rebellious, which have rebelled against me: they and their fathers have transgressed against me unto this very day; and these children are impudent and hard-hearted: I am sending thee unto them; and thou shalt say unto them, Thus saith the Lord Jehovah. And they, whether they will hear or whether they will forbear—for they are a rebellious house—yet shall they know that there hath been a prophet among them.

When the glory of the Lord appeared to Ezekiel, the call also came to him. He was called to be a prophet to the nation of Israel. And you will find the word of the Lord came to him and said, "Speak to the people, whether they hear or they forbear—for they are a rebellious people—but at least let them know that there has been a prophet among them" (see Ezekiel 2:5).

No one can see the glory of the Lord without being called to be a prophet. And, of course, I use "prophet" in the broadest sense. You remember Moses said, "Oh, that all God's people were prophets" (see Numbers 11:29). And remember Paul said, "Let all prophesy" (see I Corinthians 14:1 ff.).

In other words, there is a tremendous need today among the people of God to hear God's voice. There is a tremendous need today among God's people to see what God wants them to see. The problem today is we who are God's people, we who are supposed to see, we who are supposed to hear, we do not see, and we do not hear. We need prophetic voices in our day. But who can speak for God? Who can help God's people to see what God wants them to see? Only those who have seen the glory of the Lord. If we see the glory of the Lord, we will receive a calling. And our calling is to tell the people what is in God's mind.

What is it that God wants to convey to us? What does He see about us? And what does He want to do with us? Whether they hear or they forbear, that is not the issue. The people of God need to know that there has been a prophet among them who is speaking for God.

So, Ezekiel was called to be a prophet to his people, even though outwardly, it was almost futile since they were a rebellious nation. They would not listen. Their hearts were hardened. And yet, Ezekiel was to tell them what he saw and what he heard. In another sense, even though it did not seem to work immediately, in the long run, the prophecy of Ezekiel did have an effect. One day, there would be a remnant returning from Babylon, and I do believe, partly, it was due to the work of Ezekiel.

Dear brothers and sisters, let us not be disappointed. Whether people will hear or will forbear, we have a mission. We want to tell the people of God what we see and what we hear.

Called as a Watchman

Ezekiel 3:17—Son of man, I have appointed thee a watchman unto the house of Israel, and thou shalt hear the word from my mouth, and give them warning from me.

God not only called Ezekiel to be a prophet but also appointed him a watchman—to watch what was coming and warn the people what was to come. Hopefully, some might be rescued.

This is the same with us today. If we see the vision of God, if the glory of the Lord should appear to us, then we, too, are set up as watchmen in the church. We are to warn the people of God, and hopefully, some may be rescued.

The Glory of the Lord Appears Again

Ezekiel 8:1-3—And it came to pass in the sixth year, in the sixth month, on the fifth of the month, that as I sat in my house, and the elders of Judah sat before me, the hand of the Lord Jehovah fell there upon me. And I looked, and behold, a likeness as the appearance of fire; from the appearance of his loins and downward, fire; and from his loins and upward, as the appearance of brightness, as the look of glowing brass. And he stretched forth the form of a hand, and took me by a lock of my head; and the Spirit lifted me up between the earth and the heavens, and brought me in the visions of God to Jerusalem, to the entry of the inner gate that looketh toward the north, where was the seat of the image of jealousy, which provoketh to jealousy.

A year had passed since that open heaven vision Ezekiel had where the glory of the Lord appeared to him. It was now the sixth year of King Jehoiachin's captivity (see 1:2), and Ezekiel was among his people. The elders of Judah sat before him. Then Ezekiel looked, and behold, a likeness as the appearance of fire appeared to him, and a hand took hold of him. In the Spirit, he was lifted up and brought into Jerusalem.

Once again, the glory of the Lord appeared to Ezekiel. And that glory took him in the Spirit and brought him to Jerusalem. Why? Because there was a controversy between God and His people. There was a controversy between the glory of the Lord and the shame of His people. So, Ezekiel was brought back in the vision into Jerusalem to the house of God, and there, God wanted to show him something.

The Temple in Jerusalem

Now, this temple in Jerusalem was built by Solomon. You remember that David had such a love for God, and such a love for the house of God, that he wanted to build a house for God. If you turn to Psalm 132, you can see the heart of David. There David wrote a Psalm concerning his passion, his love for God, and for His house. He said:

> Jehovah, remember for David all his affliction; how he swore unto Jehovah, vowed unto the Mighty One of Jacob: I will not come into the tent of my house, I will not go up to the couch of my bed; I will not give sleep to mine eyes, slumber to mine eyelids, until I find out a place for Jehovah, habitations for the Mighty One of Jacob (vv. 1-4).

In the heart of David—the man who was after God's own heart—there was a passion and a longing. He longed to build God a house because, at that time, the ark of God was hidden in the woods of the forest. The ark of God was neglected. David had to find that ark.

> Behold, we heard of it at Ephratah, we found it in the fields of the wood. Let us go into his habitations, let us worship at his footstool. Arise,

Jehovah, into thy rest, thou and the ark of thy strength. Let thy priests be clothed with righteousness, and let thy saints shout for joy. For thy servant David's sake, turn not away the face of thine anointed (vv. 6-10).

It was in the heart of David to build God a house that God might enter into His rest. Remember, God had no rest because God did not have a house. The ark of God was hidden, neglected. David found it and brought the ark into the tent of David on Mount Zion. And he had a desire to build God a house. God appreciated it very much, but because he was a man that shed much blood, God said, "You are not to build it, but your son Solomon will build it" (see II Samuel 7; I Chronicles 22:7-10).

So, Solomon built the temple. It was a magnificent temple. And after the temple was finished, on the day that it was dedicated to God, fire came down from heaven and burned the burnt offering. The glory of the Lord appeared and covered the whole house, so the priests had to retreat. And all the people there, when they saw the glory of the Lord fill the house, bowed their faces to the ground, and worshiped God. They said, "Blessed be God, for His lovingkindness endures forever" (see II Chronicles 7:1-3).

What a sight! The glory of the Lord was in the house and filled the house. God was satisfied. God was satisfied with the house. God was satisfied with His people. He entered into His rest; He rested himself among His own people. Now, that was the house—the temple in Jerusalem.

About 400 years after Solomon built the temple, Ezekiel was brought back in that vision into Jerusalem to that house. But what kind of house had it become? Outwardly, it was still the same house. Outwardly, it was still glorious. It was a wonderful, beautiful edifice. Outwardly, the sacrifices were offered. Outwardly, the priesthood was functioning in the temple. Outwardly, the people who were still in Jerusalem still came to the house of God to worshipHim. Outwardly, it seemed as if nothing had changed. Everything went on as usual. But that was not the way the glory of the Lord saw His house.

Why did God bring Ezekiel back into that temple? Didn't God know what was going on in that house? Certainly, He did. But why did He bring Ezekiel back to see the situation? Remember, Ezekiel was a priest in heart. He loved God very much, and he loved the house of God. His love towards the house of God was almost like the heart of David. But why should God bring Ezekiel back to that house and show him things that would hurt Ezekiel to his very bones?

Now, why did God do that? It was as if God tried to prove a point. God was trying to show His prophet how much He was hurt by what the children of Israel did in that house. He wanted sympathy from His prophet. He wanted His prophet to stand with Him. He wanted His prophet to tell the children of Israel what the condition of the house actually was. Why? Because their eyes were blind. Even though all these things were happening for a long time, the people did not realize it. Their eyes were blind. Their ears were deaf. Their hearts were hardened. So, God wanted to show His prophet Ezekiel what the condition of the house actually was in relation to His glory. God will measure the house with His own glory to see whether the house will measure up. He wanted His prophet to see. He wanted His prophet to tell the people. Whether they hear or they forbear, it did not matter. God wanted to prove a point. God wanted to tell these people what the condition of the house was before His glory.

The Image of Jealousy

Ezekiel was brought back in that vision. There he saw the glory of the Lord. He was brought to the entry of the inner gate which "lookest toward the north." And God said to him:

> Son of man, lift up now thine eyes toward the north. And I lifted up mine eyes toward the north, and behold, northward of the gate of the altar, this image of jealousy in the entry (Ezekiel 8:5).

Remember, Ezekiel saw this in a vision. In other words, it was not necessary to have such a physical image of jealousy standing there at the entrance of the gate of the altar. There might be such an image, or there might not be such an image. And we were never told what that image of jealousy actually was because that was not important. Why? Because Ezekiel saw this in a vision. In the vision, he saw the image of jealousy there, by the entry of the altar.

What is the altar? The altar is the altar of burnt offerings. In other words, the altar is where the people of God worshiped. The altar is the place where they offered sacrifices and gifts to God. The altar is the place where the people of God devoted themselves to God. However, by the side of that altar there stood an image of jealousy. We do not know what that image of jealousy was, but we do know that our God is a jealous God. Anything that will take away the glory of God, anything that will share the glory of God, anything that would displace God—taking or sharing the place of God—is an image of jealousy. Whether it is physical and visible or spiritual and invisible, it is the same.

As the people of God, they ought to approach the altar, offer sacrifices, and give themselves to God. They ought to worship God in spirit and in truth. They ought to serve God with singleness of heart. There is only one God, and this is the one God that they should worship and serve. However, by the side of the altar was the image of jealousy.

Were they offering sacrifices on the altar to God? Were they serving God and worshiping God?

Outwardly, they might have been, but actually, inwardly they were sacrificing to an image of jealousy.

When the children of Israel were in the wilderness, what did they carry along with them in the wilderness? Was it the tabernacle of God? Was it the ark of God? Outwardly, yes, but when Stephen stood before the council and witnessed, he said that they were carrying with them their idols, because that was the reality (see Acts 7).

Oh, brothers and sisters, here you will find the people of God were outwardly offering sacrifices on the altar, but in actuality, they were worshiping idols. They had "an image of jealousy." Aside from God they worshiped something else. It might have been in the name of God, but it was not God.

When the children of Israel were at Mount Sinai as Moses went up to receive the Law, they said, "We don't know what happened to Moses." Then they came to Aaron and said, "Make us a god that will lead us." So, Aaron made a golden calf. They probably called the name of the golden calf "Jehovah." And there they worshiped the golden cow, thinking that they were worshiping God. But dear brothers and sisters, that is the image of jealousy—it is in the name of God, but not God (see Exodus 32:1-5).

And he said unto me, Son of man, seest thou what they do? the great abominations that the house of Israel commit here, to cause me to go far off from my sanctuary? (Ezekiel 8:6a)

What did God say to Ezekiel? It is as if God said, "Ezekiel, did you see what they are doing? They are driving Me away from My house. This is My house. This is My sanctuary. This is where I live. This is where I rest. This is where I am worshiped. This is where I am served, but I could not stand what they are doing there anymore. They have driven Me out. I am being driven out of My own house. Do you see that?" How it hurt God's heart!

The Chamber of Imaginations

As if this is not enough, God told Ezekiel that he would see more. God said:

And yet again, thou shalt see great abominations (Ezekiel 8:6b).

God took Ezekiel to the entry of the court and there was a wall and God said, "Dig through the wall." There was a hole, so Ezekiel dug through the wall. And behind the wall, he saw a chamber of imaginations. All kinds of beasts, creeping things, creatures were painted all around the wall. And there he saw 70 men, the elders of the nation of Israel, and they were there with censors in their hands, and they were burning incense.

The 70 elders of Israel were the leaders. They were the civil leaders of the nation of Israel. They were supposed to lead the nation to worship God. They were there in the court of God, but secretly they were worshiping their imagination. Everyone has his own imagination. One may have an imagination of a fox, the other an imagination of a snake, or the other an imagination of a crocodile. You will find everyone has his own imagination of what God is to be like. Everyone has his own concept of God, not according to revelation, not according to the word, not according to the truth, but according to his own imagination.

Dear brothers and sisters, are they burning incense to God? No! They are burning incense to their *concept* of God. Outwardly, they were burning incense to God. They were offering prayers to God. But actually, they led the nation of Israel after their imaginations far away from God.

Emotional Worship

As if this was still not enough, God said: You will yet see more abominations.

> And he brought me to the entry of the gate of Jehovah's house that was toward the north; and behold, there sat women weeping for Tammuz. And he said unto me, Seest thou; son of man? Thou shalt

yet again see greater abominations than these
(Ezekiel 8:14-15).

Here we find, at the entrance of the house of God there were women weeping for Tammuz. According to legend, he was killed every year (as the crops dried out in the sun) but then resurrected (so Spring would come). In a sense, it was a type of nature worship. In other words, these women were worshiping according to the dictates of their emotions. They worshiped as their emotions led them. It was not religion revealed by God but natural. It was emotion, but not real. God said, "You will see yet more."

Worshiping Creation

And He brought me into the inner court of Jehovah's house, and behold, at the entry of the temple of Jehovah, between the porch and the altar, were about five and twenty men, with their backs toward the temple of Jehovah and their faces toward the east; and they worshipped the sun towards the east (Ezekiel 8:16).

Here Ezekiel was brought even closer between the porch and the altar—almost into the temple itself—and he saw 25 people. Now, who were these 25 people? Some people think that since the priests served in 24 courses, and the high priest directed the 24 courses, the

25 people were probably these 24 priests along with the high priest. In other words, that was the priesthood.

The priests were in the temple serving God in the holy place. And yet, what were they doing there? They were turning their backs to God. Instead of facing the ark of God and the mercy seat, they faced the sun. Instead of worshiping the Creator, they worshiped the creation. Think of that!

Oh, brothers and sisters, it was not only the civil leaders, not only the women, but even the priests, even the religious leaders were leading the people away from God. What were the priests doing there at the temple? They were supposed to serve God in purity. Instead, they turned their backs against God. They served the creation, instead of the Creator.

God showed all these to the prophet Ezekiel, and said, "I cannot stand it anymore." How long suffering was our God! He must have suffered so much through the years. Daily He sent His prophets to His people to remind them, to show them what they actually were. But they did not listen. Even at this last hour, God raised up Ezekiel. God said, "It is hopeless, but, hope-against-hope, tell them what you saw."

Where is the Glory of the Lord?

Dear brothers and sisters, are we in a better position today? When our Lord Jesus was 30 years old, at the beginning of His public ministry, He went to the temple. This was the temple that had been rebuilt by the remnant, and beautified by King Herod. When our Lord Jesus entered into the temple area and saw the moneychangers with the cattle and sheep, He could not stand it anymore. So, He made a rope and drove the cattle and the sheep out. He overturned the table of the moneychangers. And He said, "You made My Father's house a house of merchandise." How could they do that? (see John 2:15-16).

Every year, countless people visited the temple. Every year the children of Israel came from all the corners of the earth to worship God. Every year they came to offer cattle and sheep. They paid their tribute money to the temple. And for the sake of convenience, the priests, behind the scenes, actually provided these moneychangers and these cattle and sheep that were already kosher. So, these people could just come and change their money and pay their tribute. They did not need to bring their cattle from afar; even if they did, it might not be approved. The priests had cattle that had already been approved. So, all the people needed to do was to buy them and offer them. What convenience it was, but how profitable it was to the priests too.

Nobody seemed to mind. People came in and went out, thinking that this was expedient. This was convenient. This was what it should be. This was what it must be. This was what they must live with. Nobody seemed to care.

As our Lord Jesus entered the temple, He saw what God saw. He saw what the glory of God saw. And when He saw that scene, He could not contain himself. He had to do something because it made His Father's house a house of merchandise, a bazaar.

Did they listen? They did not. After three years, at the end of the earthly ministry of our Lord Jesus, the last time He was in Jerusalem before He was crucified, He entered into the temple, and He saw that the business went on as usual. Oh, how it must hurt Him! Once again, He cleansed the temple; He overturned the tables, He drove out the cattle and said, "This is a house of prayer, and you make it a den of robbers. You are robbers." They would not have Him. They would rather have these moneychangers. They would rather have an empty temple. They did not care whether the glory of the Lord was there or not. They wanted to have Him crucified.

Oh, brothers and sisters, what are we doing today? Look at the church of God today! Do we see a beautiful building? Do we see a wonderful house? Do we see all the activities going on? Do we see all the worship going on in the name of the Lord Jesus? It is as if everything goes on as usual, as if God is worshiped and served. But where is the glory of the Lord? Is God happy? Is God satisfied? Is He worshiped? Is He served?

Oh, brothers and sisters, how we set up the image of jealousy in the very house of God! We serve according to the teaching and instruction of man, according to the imagination of our thoughts. We serve according to the traditions of the fathers. We serve out of convenience and expediency. We think that we have to live with all these things. We think that we have to have these religious things.

So, what is the house of God today? By the very side of the altar, you see the image of jealousy. In the court, you will find the chamber of imaginations. At the entrance of the house of God, you will find women weeping as if they are very religious, very emotional. They love God so much, but which God? Even the religious leaders are leading people away from worshiping God into worshiping creation.

Do we worship God in spirit and truth? Is our worship just once a week, in a certain place? The Lord said to the Samaritan woman, "The time is now. You do not worship God in Jerusalem, nor on Mount Gerizim, but he who worships God must worship Him in spirit and truth because the Father is seeking for true worshipers, those who worship Him in spirit and truth" (see John 4:23). Are we the people of God who worship God in spirit and truth?

Are we the house of God where His glory rests? Or are we just going through religious motions, doing religious activities in the name of the Lord Jesus, but one day the Lord will say, "I do not know you, you workers of lawlessness" (see Matthew 7:21-3).

Oh, that the glory of the Lord will show us what the house of God is today! If we do not see the glory of the Lord, then in our darkness, we will think that the house of God is beautiful, is wonderful. But under the light of the glory of the Lord, what will we see? It hurts God, and it should hurt us too.

Brothers and sisters, do you feel hurt, or are you satisfied? Oh, how many of God's people today are so contented because they are religious, because they are serving God ... but are they? Is the glory of God actually there? Are they really serving Him?

And what was the result? God told the prophet Ezekiel: I could not stand it anymore. I have to judge the condition of My house.

Judgment Begins with the House God

And behold, six men came from the way of the upper gate, which is turned toward the north, and every man with his slaughter weapon in his hand (Ezekiel 9:2a).

In the vision, he saw six men coming forth with slaughter weapons and another man in linen with an inkhorn. And God said to that man in linen with the inkhorn, "Go through the city. Put a mark upon the head of those who sigh and cry for the abominations that are in the temple." And that man went through the city, and he put a mark upon the foreheads of those who sigh and cry (see 9:2-4). And then God sent the six men with slaughter weapons to go and slay men and women and children, beginning from the temple. Let the temple be defiled by corpses. So, the six men started to slay the people and Ezekiel was spared. He cried, "Ah, Lord Jehovah, will you make an end of the remnant with the fury of Your wrath? Are You going to destroy Thy people all together? Will You not spare some?" (see 9:5-8).

Ezekiel was spared. Historically, Jeremiah was spared. A small remnant was spared. But the nation was destroyed.

The Scripture says, "Judgment shall begin with the house of God" (see I Peter 4:17). It is true that judgment is coming soon upon this world. One day, the world will know the wrath of the Lamb. Today, it is the patience of the Lamb, but one day the world will know the wrath of the Lamb. They shall hide themselves in caves and ask the mountains to fall upon them, because the wrath of the Lamb is come (see Revelation 6:16).

However, before judgment comes upon the world, judgment has already begun with the house of God. It is not necessarily physical killing, but spiritual. If we do not repent, we will be spiritually dead; the glory of the Lord will be departed. If we repent, we will be spared, and we shall see His glory.

Dear brothers and sisters, by the grace of God may we be among those who are spared. But who are those people? Blessed are those who weep. Blessed are those who cry because they see the abomination that is going on in the house of God in the name of Jesus (see

Matthew 7:22). Oh, what abomination! What blasphemy! Dear brothers and sisters, do you see this? Do you cry?

The Glory Departed

> And the cherubim lifted up their wings, and the wheels were beside them; and the glory of the God of Israel was over them above. And the glory of Jehovah went up from the midst of the city, and stood upon the mountain which is on the east side of the city (Ezekiel 11:22-23).

The nation of Israel was going to be judged, but the saddest thing of all was that the glory of the Lord departed from His house—the temple. This house was built for God, not for man. This house was built for the glory of God to dwell, and God was happy to dwell there. Though He was grieved and grieved, and hurt and hurt, He would not leave. But the day came when He had to leave.

If you read the four chapters in Ezekiel, from chapter eight to chapter eleven, you will find first of all, Ezekiel saw the glory of the Lord upon the throne, upon the cherubim, but the cherubim began to lift their wings. They came out of the holiest of all and rested upon the threshold of the house. God was leaving, but He lingered, not wanting to leave. He wanted to live among His people, but He was driven out. He lingered there on the threshold and then from the threshold, He was lifted up again to the east side of the court. He waited. And then, the cherubim lifted their wings, and they carried the glory of the Lord out of the city to the east side of the mountain—*Ichabod*—no glory!

Where is the glory? The glory of the Lord had departed, but even so, the glory of the Lord was in that mountain overlooking the city, overlooking the house—on the one hand, watching to see the city destroyed, the house destroyed, but on the other hand, there was a promise.

God's Promise

And I will give them one heart, and I will put a new spirit within you; and I will take away the stony heart out of their flesh, and will give them a heart of flesh; that they may walk in my statutes, and keep mine ordinances, and do them; and they shall be my people, and I will be their God (Ezekiel 11:19).

Even though God was going to destroy the city, and the house, and the people, and yet in His mercy, He spared a remnant. It was not because they were better than the rest, but because they had a broken and contrite heart. And with this remnant, God said, "I will give them a new heart, a new spirit, a heart of flesh, and they shall keep my statutes and My covenant. I will be their

God, and they will be My people." We know that this is the new covenant.

Oh, what mercy! What promise! Why? Because man may fail; God never fails. What God has in His mind from the very beginning concerning His house shall be fully realized. The grace of God, the mercy of God, will do it. Not because of man but because of God himself. Thank God, in judgment, there is mercy. May the Lord have mercy upon us.

Our heavenly Father, we are Thy people. Thou hast chosen us, even before the foundation of the world, we are chosen in Christ Jesus in love. Our Father, we are Thy house, Thy resting place, Thy home. But how we repent before Thee. We have made Thy house a house of merchandise. We have made the house of prayer a den of robbers. Oh, will Thou not come and cleanse us? Do not allow us to continue in abominations. Lord, if Thou cannot stand it, do not allow us to stand it. In spite of ourselves, oh come, Lord. Purge us, scourge us. Drive away all that which hurts Thee. Renew within us a pure heart that we may walk in Thy ways, we may keep Thy covenant, that we may be Thy people and Thou mayest be glorified in the midst of Thy own people. Lord, Thou art our only hope. We look up to Thee. Have mercy, mercy, mercy upon us! In the name of our Lord Jesus. Amen.

3—The Glory of the Lord Returned

Ezekiel 40:1-4—In the twenty-fifth year of our captivity, in the beginning of the year, on the tenth of the month, in the fourteenth year after that the city was smitten, on that same day the hand of Jehovah was upon me, and he brought me thither. In the visions of God brought he me into the land of Israel, and set me upon a very high mountain; and upon it was as the building of a city, on the south. And he brought me thither, and behold, there was a man whose appearance was like the appearance of brass, with a flax-cord in his hand, and a measuring-reed; and he stood in the gate.

And the man said unto me, Son of man, behold with thine eyes, and hear with thine ears, and set thy heart upon all that I shall shew thee; for in order that it might be shewn unto thee art thou brought hither. Declare to the house of Israel all that thou seest.

Ezekiel 43:1-12—And he brought me unto the gate, the gate which looked toward the east. And behold, the glory of the God of Israel came from the way of the east; and his voice was like the voice of many waters; and the earth was lit up with his glory. And the appearance of the vision that I saw was according to the vision that I had seen when I came to destroy the city; and the visions were like the vision that I saw by the river Chebar: and I fell upon my face. And the glory of Jehovah came into the house by the way of the gate whose front was toward the east. And the Spirit lifted me up, and brought me into the inner court; and behold, the glory of Jehovah filled the house. And I heard one speaking unto me out of the house; and a man was standing by me.

And he said unto me, Son of man, [this is] the place of my throne, and the place of the soles of my feet, where I will dwell in the midst of the children of Israel for ever; and the house of Israel shall no more defile my holy name, they nor their kings, with their fornication, and with the carcases of their kings [in] their high places, in that they set their threshold by my threshold, and their post by my post, and [there was only] a wall between me and them, and they defiled my holy name with their abominations which they committed; and I consumed them in mine anger. Now let them put away their fornication, and the carcases of their kings, far from me, and I will dwell in the midst of them for ever. Thou, son of man, shew the house to the house of Israel, that they may be confounded at their iniquities; and let them measure the pattern. And if they be confounded at all that they have done, make known to them the form of the house, and its fashion, and its goings out, and its comings in, and all its forms, and all its statutes, yea, all the forms thereof, and all the laws thereof; and write it in their sight, that they may keep the whole form thereof, and all the statutes thereof, and do them.

This is the law of the house: Upon the top of the mountain all its border round about is most holy. Behold, this is the law of the house.

In the sixth year of the captivity of Ezekiel, he was brought back to Jerusalem in the vision. There, he was shown what was going on in the holy temple. And God revealed to His prophet how the abominations that the children of Israel committed in the holy temple of God were forcing Him to leave His house.

Brothers and sisters, we have mentioned in Psalm 132, a Psalm of David, how David loved God. And because of his love for God, he desired to build God a house so that God might dwell among His people and find His resting place among His own. Then David's son Solomon built the house (see I Chronicles 28:3, 6).

However, as you read on in Psalm 132, you will find in the latter part of the Psalm the response of God towards the house:

For Jehovah hath chosen Zion; he hath desired it for his dwelling: This is my rest forever; here will I dwell, for I have desired it (vv. 13-14).

In other words, there is not only the desire for the house of God in David's heart, but in God's heart, you find the same desire. God's desire towards that house in Jerusalem was so intense. He said, "God has chosen Zion; He has desired it for His dwelling: This is My rest forever; here will I dwell, for I have desired it."

God loved this house. God had great desire for this house. He took it as His house of rest. And because of this desire of our God for His house, how reluctant He was to give up that house. That is the reason why, when He was forced to be driven out of the house of God, the glory of the Lord left the house slowly, gradually, and most reluctantly. First, the glory of the Lord upon the cherubim was lifted to the house's threshold, then from the threshold of the house, the glory of the Lord left the house and went into the court. And then from the court, the glory of the Lord upon the cherubim went out of the city to the east of the city on the mountain. That was the last that we saw the glory of the Lord in connection with His house (see Ezekiel 11:22-23).

An Empty House

After the glory of the Lord left the house, that house was an empty house. Even though outwardly, the service of the temple continued on for a number of years before it was finally destroyed, and yet, it was an empty house. Sometimes, I feel that it would be much better if that house had been destroyed right away. Why?

Because if the glory of the Lord had left that house and that house still remained, it would be a deception. Why? Because the children of Israel still went to that house. They still offered sacrifices on the altar. The priests were still serving the temple. Everything went on as usual, as if God had never left, as if this was still the house of God. They did not know that this house was now no different from any other house in the city of Jerusalem. Outwardly, it might be a bigger house, it might be a more valuable building, but in actuality, after the glory of the Lord had left that house, it was no different from any other house in the city. And yet, because that house—the temple— still stood there, oh, how the eyes of the children of Israel were blinded. They still frequented that house. They still thought that the house was the house of God. They still felt that when they went into that house, they could worship God, but God was no longer there. It was a deception. So finally, God destroyed the city. God destroyed the temple.

Dear brothers and sisters, is it not true even today? If the glory of the Lord has left the house, what is left behind is just another house. The house of God today is God's people. Maybe in the very beginning, when God's people came together, the glory of the Lord filled that house. But afterward, sometimes, as God's people begin to commit abominations, as the hearts of God's people begin to be divided, their love for God has grown cold. They have left their first love, and because they have left their first love, their love for one another has gone too.

They cannot forgive. They cannot forget. Outwardly, they may be together worshiping God, but dear brothers and sisters, if the glory of the Lord has left, it is just an empty house. It is a deception. Oh, pray that we may be awakened from that deception, that we may not think that everything is all right, everything is as it was before.

That was the problem with the church in Laodicea. They thought that everything was as rich as it was once upon a time. They even boasted of their abundance, not knowing the Lord was outside the house. He was knocking from outside. Oh, brothers and sisters, would to God that that building was destroyed, that we may not be deceived into thinking that this is the house of God.

In the 25th year of the captivity, the prophet Ezekiel had been in captivity for 25 years and by that time he was 50 years old. According to Numbers 4:47, a Levite would go into the house of God to serve when he was 30 years old, but when he was 50, he would retire. (Of course, with a prophet, there is no retirement.) However, we know that Ezekiel was a priest in heart. He was 50 years old. It was the retirement age of a priest, but to Ezekiel, it was maturity. The temple had been destroyed for 14 years already; 14 years had passed, and during those 14 years, Ezekiel continued to prophesy. But when it came to the 25th year of the captivity, when he was in his maturity, one day, the hand of the Lord came upon him and took him in the vision back to the land of Israel. He was brought back to Jerusalem to see the glory of the Lord return to the house of God. What a comfort it must be to Ezekiel!

According to history, we know that by the mercy of God, after 70 years of captivity, God called the children of Israel to go back to Jerusalem to rebuild the temple. A remnant returned and rebuilt the temple. But we have no record that they built the temple according to the vision that God had given to Ezekiel.

The Rebuilt Temple

From Ezekiel chapter 40 to chapter 43, God showed Ezekiel the house of God—the temple in Jerusalem. However, we have no proof that the remnant returning to Jerusalem rebuilt the temple according to the pattern that God showed to Ezekiel. On the contrary, the temple that the remnant rebuilt was smaller, not even comparable to the temple built by Solomon. And even before it was finished, the older people who had seen the first temple built by Solomon wept because they knew it could never be as magnificent and glorious as the temple built by Solomon. Nevertheless, a temple was built.

But in the temple rebuilt by the remnant, several things were missing:

(1) There was no ark in the holiest of all. It was empty.

(2) The glory of the Lord was not there. The glory of the Lord did not descend upon this house.

(3) No fire came down from heaven to burn the burnt offering.

(4) And there was no Urim and Thummim by which the priest could know the mind of God.

But even so, our Lord Jesus recognized this as His Father's house. You remember our Lord Jesus said, "You make My Father's house a house of merchandise" (see John 2:16).

Anyway, we know that the temple rebuilt by the remnant was not the one that God showed to the prophet Ezekiel. So, some people think that before the return of the Messiah, such a temple will be built again in Jerusalem.

Other people think probably it was not a temple to be rebuilt before the return of the Messiah, but it will be a temple rebuilt in the Millennial Kingdom. During the Millennium, there will be such a temple rebuilt. And there will be sacrifices and worship going on in that temple, according to the pattern that God showed Ezekiel.

Brothers and sisters, we know that all these earthly, material things are just shadows. That earthly, material temple in Jerusalem was a shadow, was a type. All the sacrifices that went on in the temple were shadows, were types; they were not the reality. They were there just to tell us that one day the reality would come. When we see the shadow, we know the reality is coming. But after the reality has come, then the shadow is gone. We do not hold on to the shadow once we have the reality; then we have no need of the shadow.

So, I wonder whether, in the Millennial Kingdom, there will be an actual, earthly building called the holy temple. I wonder if, during the Millennial time, there will be sacrifices—sheep and goats and bullocks—offered on the altar. I wonder: How can these things be resumed after Christ has already fulfilled all these things?

The Spiritual Reality of God's House

However, dear brothers and sisters, that does not mean that there will not be such a temple. Why? Because the temple that God showed to Ezekiel was the spiritual reality of the house of God. It was the reality that God had been after throughout the ages and the centuries. And finally, God got what He desired. He could say, "This is My rest forever. This is where I will dwell forever. I am satisfied with it" (see Psalm 132:14). And the glory of the Lord filled that house to such an extent that the earth was filled with His glory.

Oh, how we do praise and thank God that in spite of the fact that we see ruin all around, we see shortcomings all around, we see failures all around, we see distractions all around, we see emptiness all around, and yet *God is working*. The Lord Jesus said, "My Father worketh until now, and I work" (see John 5:17). Thank God that He is working! And because He is

73

working, He will get what He desires. As a matter of fact, when Ezekiel was shown the house of God, it was already completed.

Do you know, dear brothers and sisters, God has already had His house? Do you know that the city with foundations, so far as God is concerned, is already there? With God, there is no past. There is no future. There is no time factor. With God, when He desired it, He got it. But of course, so far as we are concerned, He is building it.

Our Lord Jesus said, "I will build My church upon this rock, and the gates of Hades shall not prevail against it" (see Matthew 16:18). And Abraham looked for that city with foundations whose builder is God (see Hebrews 11:10). Thank God, He is building that house. But remember, it is not a house built with dead stones. It is a house built with living stones. God is building us as His resting place.

The Way God Builds His House

Sometimes we ask this question: When and how does God build His house? Is it that God will take you, a living stone, He will take me as another living stone, and He will work upon each one of us individually? Will He carve us, embroider us, refine us, perfect us, until every living stone is a precious living stone, and after He has completed every one of us, then send us one by one to heaven to be built up together as that holy temple? Is this the way that God is building that holy temple for himself? No. The way that God is building His temple is not only today, it is not only dealing with each individual, but He is dealing with us together. He is making every one of us more and more precious. That is to say, that Christ may be formed more and more in us.

Brothers and sisters, all our preciousness is in Him. Remember, if there is any preciousness in any one of us, it is Christ. And God is working in every one of us to make every living stone into a precious stone. Some may be a sardius, some may be a sapphire, some may be emerald, some may be other precious stones. It is Christ being formed in us with many attributes of himself. It is all different, but we are all precious stones. And God is using these precious stones to build together a house for himself.

But brothers and sisters, when is He doing the building? Where is He doing the building? Right now, right where we are. If God has put us in a certain place with some brothers and sisters, this is the place. This is the time that God will not only work in each of us, but He will fit us into measure according to our brothers and sisters by our right and left sides. This is how He is building us together now. It is not that God will perfect every one of us and then send us to heaven to be built. That will be too late. If we refuse to be built up together now, we will waste our time. We will miss the opportunity.

Thank God, He could show Ezekiel the pattern of the house; it was already there. Now, of course, we know when this pattern of the temple was shown to Ezekiel, even the temple rebuilt by the remnant was not even there yet. However, so far as God is concerned, He was able to show His prophet that house because with God, the reality was already there. And how we need to catch the vision of that reality.

The Purpose for Ezekiel's Vision

Why did God show Ezekiel the house? God knew that Ezekiel loved the house of God so deeply. It must hurt him so badly when the news came that the temple was destroyed. So, God showed his servant that His house still stands. How comforting that must be! But there is a reason.

> And the man said unto me, Son of man, behold with thine eyes, and hear with thine ears, and set thy heart upon all that I shall shew thee; for in order that it might be shewn unto thee art thou brought hither. Declare to the house of Israel all that thou seest (Ezekiel 40:4).

Here you find God told Ezekiel: "Now, behold with your eyes, hear with your ears, set your heart upon all that I shall show you." In other words, what I am going to show you, you must hear very carefully, you must see it very intently, and you must put your heart wholly into it. I want you to see it so clearly. I want it to make such an impression upon you that you will never be able to forget it. And not only that, you are going to pass it on to the house of Israel, that they too may see that house.

> Thou, son of man, shew the house to the house of Israel, that they may be confounded at their iniquities; and let them measure the pattern. And if they be confounded at all that they have done, make known to them the form of the house, and its fashion, and its goings out, and its comings in, and all its forms, and all its statutes, yea, all the forms thereof, and all the laws thereof; and write it in their sight, that they may keep the whole form thereof, and all the statutes thereof, and do them (Ezekiel 43:10-11).

This house was shown to Ezekiel that he might show the pattern of this house to the house of Israel. But the house of Israel was a rebellious house. Remember, after the earthly temple of Jerusalem was destroyed and the people of Israel were taken into captivity, 14 years had passed. During these 14 years, the Spirit of God must be working in the hearts of those captives. At least, they were delivered from deception. And being in captivity, we were told that they were even delivered from idol worship. Through discipline, they were delivered from the abominations they had committed in the house before. And yet, among them, some people were confounded, puzzled. They recognized what they had done and wondered if God would ever show mercy to them again.

Furthermore, God purposely showed them the pattern of this house to confound them, to let them know what they had done. Here was the pattern of the house—holy—and when they saw that pattern, it would bring them back to what they had done to that old temple, that they would repent before God, and that they would be given a desire to do God's will.

Now, that was the reason why the pattern of that temple was shown. It was shown for a double purpose. On the one hand, it was to confound the people, to reveal to them what abominations they had done in the past, that they would repent, deeply repent. On the other hand, it was to show them the pattern so that it would create the desire in their heart for it, that their desire would be for God and for His will.

Dear brothers and sisters, you know it is relatively easy to see things negatively. We can see very quickly, very easily what is going wrong. But only seeing what is wrong will never lead us into God's purpose. I think the problem with God's people today is, of course, in general, people do not even see what is going wrong. People think that everything is going all right. Everything goes on as usual, and they do not miss anything. If that is the case, dear brothers and sisters, that is a most tragic and hopeless situation.

But thank God, among God's people today, there are some whose eyes are opened, maybe partly. They are able to see what has gone wrong in the house of God. They may begin to see the moneychangers in the temple area. They may begin to see all the buying and selling going on in the holy place. They may even begin to see the image of jealousy at the entrance of the court. They may even see hidden things that are going on in the so-called house of God.

Many people may have their eyes opened to see the negative things that are not of God. Thank God that they see. But the problem is that if all they see are the negative things, they will never be brought into that which answers to God's heart because they may leave these negative things and begin something else negative. Why? Because there is no vision of God. Where there is no vision, the people perish. Where there is no vision, the people cast off restraint. Where there is no vision, the people disintegrate.

Dear brothers and sisters, it breaks our hearts to see many who love the Lord, whose eyes are opened to see what is wrong—what is wrong here, what is wrong there. Because they see what is wrong, they leave and try to be right; yet there is no vision. And the result is that they perish. The result is that there is no restraint. The result is that they disintegrate. People who have seen negative things cannot be joined together. People who profess to love the Lord, who are willing to sacrifice, who are willing to deny themselves, who are willing to

79

be unpopular, who seem to really want to do what is right, and yet, brothers and sisters, if a person does not have vision—the pattern from above, the positive things—they can leave, but it will never be right. They can gather some people together, they can try to do what they want to, what seems right to them, but it will never be right. They will be creating more confusion. There will be more division. Why? Because they do not have vision.

The Need for Vision

The greatest need among God's people today is vision. Oh, that God will show us the pattern of His house! We need to see what God really desires, what His resting place is, what His dwelling place is, what His home that He really longs for is. We really need to see that pattern. And if we see that positive thing, brothers and sisters, we can cooperate with God. All we can do is follow and to cooperate with God. We cannot initiate anything. We cannot start anything. We cannot originate anything. Everything must come from God. That is the reason why Ezekiel was shown the pattern that he might tell the children of Israel. If they really repent of the past, and if they really want to be God's house, here is the pattern. Let them know about it that they may do the statutes and follow the Law.

Thank God, the glory of the Lord returned, but He cannot return just to any place. He can only return to the house that will satisfy Him, a house that is built according to God. "And the glory of the Lord entered from the east gate and filled the house." God said, "This is the place of my throne. This is where I put my feet. This is my resting place forever" (see Ezekiel 43:4-5, 7).

For the glory of the Lord to return, there must be a house that will answer God's heart. So, how important it is today that we see the house of God built among His people! Again, I will repeat: The building of the house of God, where His glory will rest and forever, is going on right now on earth today. Unless we allow God to build it with us and with our brothers and sisters, the glory of the Lord has no place to set His foot.

Now, of course, as we read Ezekiel chapters 40 to 43, we find the house of God was described in detail. (We will not go into details because not only spiritually, I am not adequate for it, but even technically, I do not have that engineering or architectural training to understand all the details there.)

Spiritual Principles of the House of God

Dear brothers and sisters, God showed Ezekiel the house. It is the spiritual reality of the house that is essential. And we need to see some spiritual principles embodied there in the house. In other words, these spiritual principles are the reality of the house of God. If these principles are there, we have the reality, and God has His house, and the glory of the Lord will fill that house. If we do not have these principles, then God does not have His house, and the glory of the Lord cannot fill the house. So, we will just briefly mention a few of the principles that are embodied in the pattern of the house.

One—Heavenliness

In the visions of God brought he me into the land of Israel, and set me upon a very high mountain; and upon it was as the building of a city, on the south (Ezekiel 40:2).

When Ezekiel was brought back to Jerusalem, he was brought back to a very high mountain. We know the temple that Solomon built was built on Mount Moriah. That was not a very high mountain, and yet, this house of God that God showed to Ezekiel was built on a very high mountain. It was built like a city. The immensity of that temple was like a city built upon the top of a mountain and cannot be hidden. Does that remind you of Revelation chapter 21? At the consummation of time, the holy city, the New Jerusalem, will descend from heaven. And this city was on a high mountain, high and lifted up.

What does that mean? It means elevation, spiritual elevation. Even when our Lord Jesus talked to His disciples in what we call the Sermon on the Mount, He climbed the mountain, and there He gave that sermon from the mountain. Why? Because it was not something low; it was something heavenly.

So, brothers and sisters, first of all, the house of God that is to be built is to be built on a very high mountain. It is to stay so separated from the earth. It is so high; we can say it speaks of the heavenliness of the house of God. The first principle of the house of God is heavenliness. There is nothing earthly about it. It comes out of heaven. It is heavenly.

Remember, this is what our Lord Jesus was when He was on earth. It is said that no one has ever entered heaven except the One who has come down from heaven and is still in heaven (see John 3:13). Even though our Lord Jesus was on earth, He was in heaven. He brought heaven with Him, a heavenly atmosphere around Him. Everything that came out of Him was heavenly. There was nothing earthly in Him. If this is true of Christ, it has to be true of the Body of Christ. Brothers and sisters, the first principle of the house of God is heavenliness.

Two—Measured According to Full Measurement

> And he brought me thither, and behold, there was a man whose appearance was like the appearance of brass, with a flax-cord in his hand, and a measuring-reed; and he stood in the gate (Ezekiel 40:3).

We find a man there, a man with the appearance of shining brass. Brass in the Scripture usually speaks of judgment. He had in his hand a flax-cord (a linen tape) and a measuring-reed (a measuring rod), which is six cubits long (see v.5).

In other words, here was a man who had in his hand two instruments for measuring. One was a linen tape to measure longer distances. The other was a rod of six cubits, which was to measure shorter measurements. And this man, whose appearance was like brass, was to measure everything in that house of God. Not only the walls around the house of God, not only the gates of it, but even the pavement and everything—big and small. He would measure to see that everything was according to its right measurement. And the one who measured it was a man with the appearance of brass.

Now, we think that this man with the appearance of brass is our Lord Jesus. You remember our Lord Jesus said: The Father does not judge anyone, but He has given judgment to the Son. So, our Lord Jesus is God's instrument of judging everything. He will measure everything. He *is* the measurement. He will measure everything according to himself.

Brothers and sisters, if the Lord is measuring us today, and He is, do not wait until that day when we shall appear before the judgment seat of Christ and then have our work tested by fire. That is a little too late. Let us live today under the light of the judgment seat of Christ.

In Revelation chapter one, our Lord Jesus was that Son of Man, who was walking in the midst of the seven golden lampstands. Our Lord Jesus today is this Man with the appearance of brass. He is walking in our midst. He is measuring you and measuring me. He is measuring us together. He measures us to see if we measure up to His standard.

Dear brothers and sisters, there is only one standard—Christ himself. He will not measure us with how much we know mentally. He does not measure us by how active we are or how passive we are. He will measure us with himself—how much of himself is being constituted and incorporated into our lives. It is the measure of Christ. It is the measure of the stature of Christ. It is the measure of the fullness of the stature of Christ.

Oh, brothers and sisters, one day we will find in that house everything is measured to its full measurement. It is the measure of the fullness of the stature of Christ. In Ephesians 4:13, we are told: "Until we all arrive at the unity of the faith and of the knowledge of the Son of God, at the full-grown man, at the measure of the stature of the fullness of Christ." That is what the measurement is.

But today, He is measuring us to see if His life in us measures up to His measurement. If it does not, He will deal with us. He may adjust us somewhat here or there. He is doing that work in our lives so that we will come up to that measurement, and every one of us will be fitted, one with another. When that house is built, it is the measure of the fullness of the stature of Christ.

Do you allow Him to measure you today? If you do not come up to His measurement—because of His love for you and for the house—He will begin to chastise you, to discipline you, to child-train you. Will you rebel? Are you willing to let Him mold and fashion you? Oh, how we need to be molded and fashioned. Are we willing to let Him do the necessary work in us? Remember, the house of God is the full measurement of Christ.

Three—Holiness

A wall separated the whole temple area from the rest of the land. The first thing you saw would be the wall; there was a wall all around the holy place. It is 500 reeds, approximately a mile long and a mile wide. The whole area was surrounded by a wall about 12 feet thick and 12 feet high. But as you read these chapters, you find that the most interesting thing is that you have more than one wall in this temple building.

In the Garden of Eden, there was no wall. And because there was no wall, the problem came. But this temple was surrounded by a wall, not only one wall that marked the border of the holy place—500 square reeds (or, 3000 square cubits)—but there was another wall for the outer court—500 square cubits. And there was another wall for the inner court—100 square cubits. There are three walls, one within another. Why? Again, we will find that it is not the physical or the technical thing that is important. The reason why there is a wall, and another wall, and another wall is because there is a principle God is trying to impress upon us. And what is that principle? These walls represent one principle: it is the principle of being holy.

> This is the law of the house: Upon the top of the mountain all its border round about is most holy. Behold, this is a law of the house (Ezekiel 43:12).

You know, the opposite of righteousness is sin, but the opposite of holiness is commonness. Anything common is not holy. Oftentimes, we think of holy as the opposite of sin—if it is sinful, it is unholy. Of course, if it is sinful, it is unholy. But strictly speaking, if it is sinful, it is unrighteous. If it is common, then it is unholy. Our God is holy.

Oh, brothers and sisters, these living creatures were crying out day and night, unceasingly: "Holy, holy, holy, Lord God Almighty." Do you know what that means? It means that our God is holy. He is not common. He is different. He is unique. He is all alone. There is none like Him. That is the law of the house. Nothing common can enter the house of God.

The controversy of God with the children of Israel was that in the past, they allowed the common, the uncircumcised, the strangers to enter into God's court and defile God's place. But this house of God, that God would dwell in forever is surrounded by wall after wall and wall after wall. That is to say, everything that is common has been kept out. Anything uncircumcised, anything strange, is kept out. Within the whole area, it is most holy.

The only way we can explain the word *holy* is that all around the border, we see God himself. There is nothing of man. Everything is of God. All things are of God. When John was shown the holy city, God told him, "Behold, I make all things new" (Revelation 21:5). There is nothing old, nothing common, not to mention nothing sinful.

Often our whole approach is: Is it sinful? If it is not a sin, then it is all right. But brothers and sisters, it is not all right. Because God will ask: Is it holy? Is it of Me? Is it an expression of what I am? God is very jealous over that matter. And that is the reason why, when Peter said, "It is good to be here with Moses, with Elijah, and with your Christ," God said, "No, I am holy. I am alone—not Moses, nor Elijah, but My Son. Hear Him." This is the law of the house.

Brothers and sisters, are we holy because He is holy? There is only one reason why we must be holy, and we find it in Leviticus. God required His people to be holy, and there is only one reason. The reason is, as God said, "I am holy."

Oh, that we may be delivered from all that which is common, all that which is of the world, all that which is of man, that even in the border, the wall all around the city, it may be most holy, separated unto God.

Four—Death and Resurrection

It is very strange that as you read, you will find there is a very detailed description of the gates (see Ezekiel 41). The gates can seem complicated since we normally think of a single gate entrance through a threshold. But these gates mentioned are actually part of a gate building. There are gates to the holy place, gates to the outer court, gates to the inner court, and gates to the house of God. This gated structure includes more than one set of gates. It has an outer threshold. As you go over an outer threshold, you enter a hallway with guard rooms on two sides and spaces in between. And when you come to the other end, there will be an inner threshold. And as you cross the inner threshold, you will get into a porch. And there are columns there. It is very elaborate.

Now, thank God for all these gates because if there is a wall without gates, it is a prison. This is why all these gates are there. Without going into detail, these gates by which people enter in, of course, are Christ. The Lord Jesus said, "I am the door." It is Christ. And these gates represent the death and resurrection of our Lord Jesus. That is how we get into the house of God. It is through the death and the resurrection of our Lord Jesus. There is no other door.

How do we come into the house of God? By Christ, by His death and resurrection. But remember, His death and resurrection are all-inclusive. In other words, it is not only that through His death and resurrection, we may have our sins forgiven and receive eternal life. That is true. But His death and resurrection also include you and me. Not only has He borne our sin in His body, but even you and me He has taken with Him, and in Him crucified. In His resurrection, He not only released His life to us that we may have life, but we are raised together with Him. "No longer live I, but it is Christ (see Galatians 2:20). That is the only way to enter into the house of God. We cannot enter into the house of God if we do not know the death and resurrection of our Lord Jesus in experience. We cannot enter into the house of God if, what we would say, we are not saved. But even moreso, if we really want to be the house of God, brothers and sisters, we must die. It is only on resurrection ground—after death—that the house is built.

Five—Fellowship

Then, there is the outer court, the inner court, and the house itself. In the outer court, there are pavements, and there are cells. Now, people believe that these 30 cells probably are used for the children of Israel to cook and to eat the peace offerings, the sacrifices. That is the place where they can eat. So, the outer court, spiritually speaking, is the place where God's people enjoy Christ.

They know Christ as their sacrifice. They know Christ as their peace. And because of that, they commune with Christ, they feed upon Christ, and they enjoy Christ spiritually. And by enjoying and feeding upon Christ, they are strengthened. They are able to walk in their pilgrimage. Dear brothers and sisters, that is what we must have. By God's grace, we who have entered into the court are to enjoy our Christ. We are to feed upon Him. And only by doing that are we strengthened spiritually that we may be able to walk our way and finish our course.

Then, we come to the inner court and find there are cells there. But these cells are not for the children of Israel. These cells are for the priests and for those who take charge of the altar. And in the inner court, we will find the altar there. So, what does it mean? It means that we are not only believers in the outer court who enjoy Christ as our nourishment, but we are also priests unto God. Now remember this, it is not that some children of God are priests and some are not. No. Spiritually speaking, in the new covenant, every believer is a priest. So, we first enjoy Christ, then as we all are strengthened, we enter into the inner court, and we begin to function as priests. We begin to minister in the house of God. But in the inner court, we are ministering more unto the house and unto the people, than unto God himself.

Then, we enter into the holy place, the house itself. And in the house, there is the table of the Lord. Actually, the table of the Lord is an altar of wood. You know, in the tabernacle built by Moses, there was the golden altar of incense and the golden table of shewbread. But here it is strange because in the house we find there is a table, but that table is the altar. In other words, the altar and the table come together. It is both the altar and the table. Why? Because it speaks of how we begin to minister unto the Lord himself. We do not just minister to the house, to the people of God, but we minister unto the Lord.

And of course, in the holiest of all, there is the glory of the Lord. And the glory of the Lord not only dwells in the holiest of all, but it also breaks out into the rest of the house: into the holy place, into the inner court, into the outer court, and it fills the earth.

Brothers and sisters, this is what God desires to have. And remember, it is not without you and me. It is to be, not only *with* you and me, but *in* you and *in* me. Will we allow Him to build that house?

Our heavenly Father, we do praise and thank Thee because Thou didst show thy servant Ezekiel that house, Thy resting place which Thou desired through the ages and centuries, and how Thou took delight in it. Oh, our Father, we do pray that by Thy Holy Spirit, Thou wilt give us wisdom and revelation to see that house that Thou lovest so much. Oh, it is a glorious church, without spot or wrinkle or any of such sort, holy without blemish, the bride of the Lamb, the resting place of God. Lord, show us that we may be constrained to give ourselves to Thee and allow Thee to work it out in and among us, to Thy heart's satisfaction that the glory of the Lord may fill the house. We ask in Thy precious name. Amen.

4—The Restoration of Priesthood and Kingship

Ezekiel 44:1-31—And he brought me back toward the outer gate of the sanctuary which looked toward the east; and it was shut. And Jehovah said unto me, This gate shall be shut; it shall not be opened, and no one shall enter in by it: for Jehovah, the God of Israel, hath entered in by it; and it shall be shut. As for the prince, he, the prince, shall sit in it to eat bread before Jehovah: he shall enter by the way of the porch of the gate, and shall go out by the way of the same.

And he brought me the way of the north gate before the house; and I beheld, and lo, the glory of Jehovah filled the house of Jehovah: and I fell upon my face. And Jehovah said unto me, Son of man, apply thy heart, and behold with thine eyes, and hear with thine ears all that I say unto thee concerning all the statutes of the house of Jehovah, and all the laws thereof; and mark well the entering in of the house, with every going forth of the sanctuary; and say to the rebellious, to the house of Israel, Thus saith the Lord Jehovah: Let it suffice you of all your abominations, O house of Israel, in that ye have brought strangers, uncircumcised in heart and uncircumcised in flesh, to be in my sanctuary, to profane it, [even] my house, when ye offered my bread, the fat and the blood; and they have broken my covenant besides all your abominations. And ye have not kept the charge of my holy things, but have set keepers of my charge in my sanctuary for yourselves.

Thus saith the Lord Jehovah: No stranger, uncircumcised in heart and uncircumcised in flesh, shall enter into my sanctuary, of any stranger that is among the children of Israel. But the Levites who went away far from me, when Israel went astray, going astray from me after their idols, they shall even bear their iniquity; but they shall be ministers in my sanctuary, having oversight at the gates of the house, and doing the service of the house: they shall slaughter the burnt-offering and the sacrifice for the people, and they shall stand before them to minister unto them. Because they ministered unto them before their idols, and were unto the house of Israel a stumbling-block of iniquity; therefore have I lifted up my hand against them, saith the Lord Jehovah, that they shall bear their iniquity. And they shall not draw near unto me, to do the office of a priest unto me, nor to draw near to any of my holy things, [even] to the most holy; but they shall bear their confusion, and their abominations which they have committed. And I will make them keepers of the charge of the house, for all the service thereof, and for all that shall be done therein.

But the priests, the Levites, the sons of Zadok, that kept the charge of my sanctuary when the children of Israel went astray from me, they shall approach unto me to minister unto me, and they shall stand before me to present unto me the fat and the blood, saith the Lord Jehovah. They shall enter into my sanctuary, and they shall approach unto my table, to minister unto me, and they shall keep my charge. And it shall come to pass when they enter in at the gates of the inner court, they shall be clothed with linen garments; and no wool shall come upon them, when they minister in the gates of the inner court, and towards the house. They shall have linen tires upon their heads and shall have linen breeches upon their loins; they shall not gird on anything that causeth sweat. And when they go forth into the outer court, into the outer court to the people, they shall put off their garments wherein they ministered, and lay them in the holy cells; and they shall put on other garments, that they may not hallow the people with their garments. Neither shall they shave their heads, nor suffer their locks to grow long: they shall duly poll their heads. Neither shall any priest drink wine when they enter into the inner court. And they shall not take for their wives a widow, nor her that is put away; but they shall take maidens of the seed of the house of Israel, or a widow that is the widow of a priest. And they shall teach my people [the difference] between holy and profane, and cause them to discern between unclean and clean. And in controversy they shall stand to judge: they shall judge it according to my judgments; and they shall keep my laws and my statutes in all my solemnities; and they shall hallow my sabbaths. And they shall come at no dead person to become unclean; but for father, or for mother, or for son, or for daughter, for brother, or for sister that hath had no husband, they may become unclean. And after he is cleansed, they shall count unto him seven days. And on the day that he goeth into the sanctuary, unto the inner court, to minister in the sanctuary, he shall present his sin-offering, saith the Lord Jehovah. And it shall be unto them for an inheritance; I am their inheritance: and ye shall give them no possession in Israel; I am their possession. They shall eat the oblation and the sin-offering and the trespass-offering; and every devoted thing in Israel shall be theirs. And the first of all the first-fruits of every [kind], and every heave-offering of every [kind], of all your heave-offerings, shall be for the priests; ye shall also give unto the priest the first of your dough, that he may cause the blessing to rest on thy house. The priests shall not eat of anything that dieth of itself, or of that which is torn, whether of fowl or of beast.

Ezekiel 45:7-10—And the prince shall have [his portion] on from the one side and on the other side of the holy heave-offering and of the possession of the city, over against the holy heave-offering, and over against the possession of the city, from the west side westward, and from the east side eastward; and in length answering to one of the portions [of the tribes] from the west border unto the east border. As land shall it be his for a possession in Israel; and my princes shall no more oppress my people; but they shall give the land to the house of Israel according to their tribes.

Thus saith the Lord Jehovah: Let it suffice you, princes of Israel! Put away violence and spoil, and execute judgment and justice; take off your exactions from my people, saith the Lord Jehovah. Ye shall have just balances, and a just ephah, and a just bath.

Ezekiel 45:17—And it shall be the prince's part [to supply] the burnt-offerings, and the oblation, and the drink-offering, at the feasts, and at the new moons, and on the sabbaths, in all the solemnities of the house of Israel: it is he that shall prepare the sin-offering, and the oblation, and the burnt-offering, and the peace-offerings, to make atonement for the house of Israel.

Our heavenly Father, we do praise and thank Thee for Thy written word. We just ask that at this moment the Spirit of God will breathe upon Thy word and make it living and operative in each of our lives. Oh, how we praise and thank Thee because Thy word is living. Thy word is even life and spirit to us. So, we just look to Thee to release Thy word and release us for Thy word. Oh, that we may see Thy glory. In the name of our Lord Jesus. Amen.

The prophet Ezekiel was in the land of captivity. In the beginning of the book of Ezekiel, he was 30 years old. This was the time that, as a priest, he was to enter into the holy temple to serve the Lord, but his situation was just impossible. He was not in the land of Israel; he was exiled in Babylon. He was not able to go to the temple in Jerusalem. He was by the River Chebar. He was not able to enter into the temple to serve as a priest unto God. He was a slave laborer among the captives by the River Chebar, and there was no prospect for him to return to Jerusalem to do the work that he had been training for all his life. He was not only trained to serve as a priest, but he loved the priestly ministry from the very bottom of his heart. You can understand the despair, the disappointment, the emptiness, the frustration, the very sentence of death upon that person.

But thank God, it was at this most unusual time, under the most unusual circumstances, that the heavens were opened to him, and he saw the visions of God.

Dear brothers and sisters, when this happened to him, it transformed his life. It gave meaning to his life. It gave him a mission to fulfill. He was called to be a prophet, a prophet-priest. Even though he could not serve in Jerusalem in the temple that Solomon built, he was called to serve among the captives in Babylon. Life became real, living, meaningful, purposeful. All his problems were solved. It was all because he now lived under an open heaven. He saw. He saw the glory of the Lord.

Dear brothers and sisters, is this not what we need? We need to live under an open heaven. We need to see the visions of God. Oh, if only the glory of the Lord would appear to us, all our frustrations, all our despair, all our problems, all our emptiness would be gone. We will find ourselves, as it were, absorbed into that glory of the Lord. And we will find ourselves not only in union but in cooperation with God.

When the glory of the Lord appeared, the call came to Ezekiel. He was called to be a prophet. He was to tell the children of Israel what he saw and what he heard. And he was called to be a watchman standing on a high place to warn the people of what was coming that perchance he might be able to save some from destruction.

Today, if it should please the Lord that He give you an open heaven and the vision of God, and the glory of the Lord shall appear to you, remember, you have a call. You have a responsibility. You are to tell the children of God what you have seen and heard. You are to warn the people, and maybe by the grace of God, some may be rescued.

We find that even when the glory of the Lord departed from the temple, even when the judgment of God came upon that city, some were spared. A remnant was spared. And how we look to the Lord that even today as the church is going through judgment—we believe that the house of God is already in judgment—but in the time of judgment, that a remnant might be spared. Oh, would to God, that we may be among that remnant. It is not because we are better than anybody else that we might be that remnant. No, we have sinned and sinned terribly, just like the rest, but somehow, by His mercy, we cried out, we moaned over the abominations that we had committed. In other words, we repented. Because we have repented, God showed mercy to us in the time of judgment.

We have mentioned that in the 25th year of the captivity, by that time Ezekiel was 50 years old. But thank God, before Ezekiel passed off of the scene, he received such mercy from God, that in the Spirit he was lifted and was transported into Jerusalem again. And while he was there, instead of seeing a city in ruin, instead of seeing the holy temple completely destroyed, he saw a very high mountain. And on that mountain, he saw the temple—the house—like a city. And the glory of the Lord entered into the house and filled it.

We do believe that it is the will of God that in spite of what happened on earth, in spite of change and decay all around us, in spite of the falling away, in spite of the love among God's people growing cold, yet God intends to show us that He still has His house. And dear brothers and sisters, God intends to show us what a house it is! God intends to show us that His glory shall fill that house. God intends to tell us that this is the place of His throne. This is the place where He puts the sole of His feet. This is His dwelling place among His people forever.

Dear brothers and sisters, this is a vision that we must have. If we do not see this vision, we easily give up. If we do not see this vision, there is no meaning for our existence upon this earth. If we have not this vision, we may struggle and strive, but no matter what we do, it will not accomplish what God wants. But thank God, it is in the midst of all this depression and despair, disappointment and ruin, falling away and growing cold that God will give us a vision of the house of God, which He has in His mind from time eternal.

Even before God created the heavens and the earth, in eternity past before time began, God had that house in His heart, a dwelling place for himself, a home, an eternal home where He could rest among his people. Dear brothers and sisters, this has never changed. It remains the same from the beginning to the end, from eternity past, through time, into eternity to come. It is always there before God, and it is completed. And the glory of God fills the house. That is, God is fully satisfied with that house.

Brothers and sisters, we need that vision. Without that vision, we perish. Without that vision, we cast off all restraint. Without that vision, we just disintegrate. And that is what we will find today among God's people, how we are being disintegrated—just falling apart. But that vision will unite us together. That vision will give us a goal. That vision will give us direction. That vision will give us strength to press on.

Brothers and sisters, do we see that house? It is heavenly. Everything in that house measures up to the full measurement of Christ. The border all around is most holy; nothing is common. It is separated with several walls protecting it. There are gates that enter into that place, which signify the death and resurrection of our Lord Jesus. There is fellowship. And then, not only can we enjoy Christ, but we can minister to God's people, and we can even minister to the Lord. We need to have that vision.

Now, we would like to continue and to conclude. We find that in Ezekiel chapters 44 to 48. After God had shown Ezekiel that completed house, the glory of the Lord entered from the east gate and just filled the house. That is to say, God took possession of His house; God now rested in His house.

Then in Ezekiel chapter 44, God brought Ezekiel back toward the outer gate of the sanctuary which looked toward the east. Ezekiel was brought back to the east gate. And he found that the gate was shut. Why? Because that was the gate where the glory of the Lord would enter into that house (see vv. 1-2). And after the glory of the Lord entered into the house, that gate was to be shut again. No one was to enter in or to go out except the prince (see v. 3).

Then, Ezekiel was brought into the court through the north gate. And when he got into the court, what did he see? He said, "I beheld, and lo, the glory of Jehovah filled the house of Jehovah: and I fell upon my face" (Ezekiel 44:4). Once again, he saw the glory of the Lord.

Priesthood and Kingship

Brothers and sisters, whenever one sees the glory of the Lord, invariably, he falls upon his face. And this is what Ezekiel did. He fell upon his face, and then he heard God speak. God spoke to him that he might speak to the house of Israel. The restoration of the house of God is not complete if priesthood and kingship are not fully restored. In other words, priesthood and kingship are part of the house of God.

So here, the glory of the Lord began to deal with this matter of the restoration of priesthood and kingship in order to complete the restoration of the house of God. The glory of the Lord was to measure priesthood, was to measure kingship. The glory of the Lord was to bring priesthood into what it ought to be. And the glory of the Lord will bring kingship into what it was ordained to be. So, God was calling his people to return to priesthood and kingship as He ordained such to be.

In the book of Revelation 1:5b-6 it says,

> To him who loves us, and has washed us from our sins in his blood, and made us a kingdom, priests to his God and Father: to him be the glory and the might to the ages of ages. Amen.

Here is a declaration: "To Him who loves us." Oh, to God who loves us! And because He loves us, He does something to us. He has washed us from our sins in His blood. Now, thank God for this, that our sins were all washed clean. He has washed us from our sins by His precious blood. We cannot thank God enough for what He has done for us. He has forgiven our sins, He has washed our sins away, not just covered them, but washed them away. He will not only forgive but forget; it is all gone. We are clean before God. How we thank God for what He has done!

But dear brothers and sisters, that is just the beginning. He has not only washed us from our sins in

His blood, but He has made us a kingdom. Or, to put it in another way: He has made us kings and priests to His God and Father (see Revelation 5:10). Do we know that we are not just saved, but we are saved to be priests and kings unto God?

And then again, if you read Revelation 5, you find when the living creatures and the elders fell before the Lamb, they began to sing a new song. And in that new song, it says,

> ... because thou hast been slain, and hast redeemed to God, by thy blood, out of every tribe, and tongue, and people, and nation, and made them to our God kings and priests; and they shall reign over the earth (vv. 9b-10).

Oh, how glorious it is that the blood of our Lord Jesus has bought us unto God from every tribe, every tongue, every nation, every people, and He has done it, and He is doing it! He has not only purchased us by His blood but also made us kings and priests unto God, that we shall reign with Him over the earth.

In I Peter 2:5, it says that as we come to Christ, we become "living stones, [that] are being built up a spiritual house, a holy priesthood, to offer spiritual sacrifices acceptable to God by Jesus Christ." We who are redeemed of the Lord, we are living stones. And these living stones are to be built up together into a spiritual house. It is not the will of God that these living stones should be scattered all around as ruins. It is not the will of God that these living stones are just piled upon each other. And do you know this is what we are doing? We say these living stones should not be scattered, so we just pile them together into piles and piles of living stones. But God cannot live in these piles. These living stones have to be built up together. There must be an organic work going on.

Dear brothers and sisters, we have seen lots of mechanical work going on, but we see very little organic work going on. We have seen many human efforts piling people together, but we see very little of the work of the Holy Spirit in building His people, knitting His people, joining His people, uniting His people, connecting His people to where each one finds his place.

Oh, brothers and sisters, this is what our Lord is doing today: "I will build My church." Nobody can do it. He alone can do it. And He is doing it by the power of the Holy Spirit, but He needs our cooperation. If we resist, if we refuse, He will not force us. If we flee, if we escape, He has to wait until we are willing to come back and put ourselves under His hand.

The Priesthood

We are being built up together into a spiritual house, but dear brothers and sisters, what will that house be like if there is not a holy priesthood?

Remember when Moses finished building and setting up the Tabernacle? He set up the curtains, he put all the pieces of furniture in the tabernacle, and everything was ready. But there was no movement. It was not until the priests entered the Tabernacle and began to serve that the whole house was living and God was glorified.

Dear brothers and sisters, we are not only a holy temple, the house of God, but at the same time we are a holy priesthood. Remember, every believer is a priest. Even during the time of the Reformation, Martin Luther actually preached the universal priesthood of believers, but it was not accepted. The glory of the Lord will fully recover the priesthood. If priesthood is not recovered, God will never be satisfied. That is the reason why the glory of the Lord appeared and the call came to God's people. God said, "I want to see my priesthood recovered and recovered to the fullest."

In the beginning, when God brought the children of Israel out of Egypt into Mount Sinai, God said, "I have brought you unto Me as on eagle's wings. If you keep My commandments and My covenant, I will make you a people for myself, out of all nations. And I will make you a nation of priests. You will be My people, and I will be your God" (see Exodus 19:4-6).

It was God's original purpose that the whole nation of Israel was to be a nation of priests—all the men, all the women, all the children—everyone that was born into the house of Israel was a priest. And a priest was one who served God. That was God's purpose. But unfortunately, when Moses was receiving the Ten Commandments on Mount Sinai, the children of Israel sinned against God. And because they sinned, they disqualified themselves from the service of God. As an emergency measure, God took one house, the house of Aaron, one tribe, the tribe of Levi, to be priests for the house of Israel. If any child of Israel wanted to worship God, wanted to draw near to God, wanted to offer sacrifices, or even offer gifts, they could not do it themselves. They had to go through the priests. There was an intermediary between them and God. However, that was not God's original purpose.

Since our Lord Jesus completed the work of redemption, He has brought us back to the beginning. He has brought us back to the very purpose of God for the redeemed, and that purpose of God is that every redeemed child of God is a priest. Dear brothers and sisters, we are priests. You and I are priests by birth. We are priests by vocation. Our lives are to serve God. Our lives are to serve God's purpose. This is what we are. It is the universal priesthood of believers.

But when God spoke to the house of Israel through Ezekiel, God said:

> Say to the rebellious, to the house of Israel, Thus saith the Lord Jehovah: Let it suffice you of all your abominations, O house of Israel, in that ye have brought strangers, uncircumcised in heart and

uncircumcised in flesh, to be in my sanctuary, to profane it, even my house, when ye offered my bread, the fat and the blood; and they have broken my covenant besides all your abominations. And ye have not kept the charge of my holy things, but have set keepers of my charge in my sanctuary for yourselves (Ezekiel 44:6-7).

In other words, God was telling them what they did before. God said, "You have brought in strangers, uncircumcised in heart and in flesh to profane my sanctuary." Maybe physically, outwardly, the children of Israel never did that. Remember, even in the time of Paul, when Paul was suspected of bringing some Gentiles into the house of God, immediately there was a riot. Why? Because there was a sign on the wall of the women's court saying that no Gentile could cross this place. If anyone should cross this wall, he should die.

Outwardly, the children of Israel were very strict by not allowing any stranger, any uncircumcised people to enter into the house of God, but they themselves were strangers to God. They themselves were uncircumcised in heart. They were those who profaned the house of God. And when the children of Israel went away from God, the Levites went away with them. The Levites, who were supposed to serve in the house of God, were serving the idols that the people wanted. Or, possibly, the Levites even led the people into idol worship. Oh, what a falling away!

When there was a falling away, when the house of God was profaned by the people of God, when they were worshiping the idols of their imaginations, oh, even the Levites were led astray. In their eagerness to serve the people, they followed the people. They catered to the wishes of the people. Whatever the people wanted, they would do.

You may think that this will not happen. It happened. Remember? When the people told Aaron, "Make us a god. We do not know what has happened to this Moses that has brought us up out of the land of Egypt. We cannot see the God he told us about. We want something tangible, something we can see, something we can hold. Make us a god." Oh, Aaron made the golden calf for them and proclaimed a holy day (see Exodus 32:1-5).

Brothers and sisters, do you not know that this is happening even today? We are Levites. We are a people who ought to serve God, but how often we listen to what people say. We let them have what they want. We want to please man instead of God.

And because of that, in the restoration of the priesthood, God said that the Levites should bear their iniquity (see Ezekiel 44:10). Yes, they could enter into the court. They could serve the people. They could help in killing the sacrifices. They could do all the services of the house, but they could not serve as priests in the inner court. They could minister to the house of God, but they could not minister to God.

In the beginning, there was no distinction between ministering unto the house and ministering unto God. The priests were called to minister to the people of God and to minister to God. There was no distinction between these two parts of priestly functions. But because of the failure, when there was a falling away, the Levites fell away. Therefore, they could only minister to the house of God; they could not minister to God himself.

When the children of Israel fell away, and even the Levites fell away, only the house of Zadok of the priesthood stood faithful to the charge of the Lord. They were the minority. They were just a few. They stood against the tide. They were unpopular. Probably they bore much shame and reproach. They were considered the outcasts, dust, but they stood firm, faithful to God. And God said, "In My house, the household of Zadok shall be priests. They shall enter into My sanctuary and minister unto Me" (see Ezekiel 44:15-16).

Ministry unto the House of God

Brothers and sisters, what is the difference between ministering unto the house of God and ministering unto the God of the house? What is the house of God today? The house of God is God's people. Certainly, we should minister to God's people. But often, when we minister to God's people, we end up being people-oriented. Our ministry is motivated or governed by their needs. We see need here; we see need there. We see needs among God's people, and as we see all these needs, we feel we have to rush here and there in order to supply these needs, to help God's people.

When an Israelite came to offer a bullock, he himself was not able to bind the bullock. He is not able to kill the bullock. So, the Levites would come and bind the bullock, kill the bullock, and do all the things to prepare for the sacrifice. Certainly, that service is necessary and very much needed. However, ministering unto the house of God is people-oriented, and it is governed by needs.

How much of the so-called service unto the Lord is people-oriented today? It is not because we hear God but because we hear people. It is not because God said, "You go," it is because people said, "Here is the need." Now, of course, these needs should be met. Of course, the people should be served. But if we only minister to the house of God, if we minister because of the needs, the result will be that we help them by the energy of our flesh. There is no need to wait upon the Lord. There is no need to seek the mind of the Lord. There is no need to cast ourselves upon the power from on high. We can just minister to what we see, and we just minister with what we have—our talents, our ability, our cleverness, our experience. We can do it. We don't need God. And oftentimes, when we are doing that, probably, we will be troubled. There is no rest in our soul.

Ministry to the Lord First

Oh, it is like Martha. She was so busy that she was really troubled. She complained to the Lord. She was unhappy with her sister. And is it not true? Oh, that we may not only minister to God's people, the house of God, but like Mary, we should first minister unto the Lord himself.

How much ministry today is just a horizontal relationship from people to people? But we need our service to be, shall I say, parabolic. We have to go up and come down. We need to minister unto the Lord first, and then out of that ministry comes the ministry unto the house of God.

Remember the church in Antioch? In Acts chapter 13, there were five prophets and teachers, and they were together. (I love this.) It says, "They were ministering to the Lord" (v. 2). These were prophets and teachers. Prophets are to speak to the people; teachers are to instruct the people. Certainly, they should be people-oriented. But no, here they ministered unto the Lord because if they do not, what can they speak to the people? Out of their own imagination? Out of their own research? Oh, how all our ministries should begin with ministering unto the Lord! In the full restoration of the priesthood, God will be ministered unto first, and even the people will be ministered unto. That is priesthood.

What is Ministry Unto the Lord?

One—Stand Before the Lord

... they shall approach unto me to minister unto me, and they shall stand before me (Ezekiel 44:15b).

The first thing in ministry unto the Lord is to stand. We think of ministry as to run. We have to run; run hither and thither. Oh, the needs are so great! Brothers and sisters, you may burn yourself out, and you cannot meet all the needs. You may run until you drop dead—and many did drop dead—the mortality of ministry is very high. Oh, that we may learn how to stand before the Lord! "Be still and know that I am God" (Psalm 46:10).

To stand is to stand as a servant. *To stand* is not to stand idle. *To stand* is not to be passive. *To stand* is actively passive. Why? Because a servant as he stands before his master, his eyes are upon his master. He is waiting on his master. Maybe even waiting for his master to just wave his hand, and he knows what his master wants. Maybe his master would just cast his eyes. He catches the eyes of his master, and he knows what his master wants (see Psalm 123:2). In other words, he is waiting there with expectancy. He will not move until the master says, "Move."

Dear brothers and sisters, it is hard for the flesh to stand still. May we stand before God, and wait upon Him until we receive word from Him, either with a distinct word, or with a wave of the hand or even with a signal of the eyes. That is ministry unto the Lord. Before you go to the people, do you first wait upon Him?

Two—Present the Fat and the Blood

> ... to present unto Me the fat and the blood, saith the Lord Jehovah (Ezekiel 44:15c).

The priests offered the fat of the sacrifice and the blood of the sacrifice unto the Lord. Now, what is the blood? The blood represents the atoning death of our Lord Jesus. Oh, thank God, when our Lord Jesus was crucified on the cross and His blood was shed, the blood has atoning power in it. The blood washes our sins away. The blood cleanses us. That is the blood.

What is the fat? The fat shows us that the life of the sacrificial animal was abundant. When you have more than you need to sustain through the day, what is left over becomes fat. So the fat on a sacrifice shows the abundance of life. I know that we don't like fat today, but in the scriptures, fat speaks of an abundant life.

So here again, how we need the atoning death of our Lord Jesus—the blood. And the death of our Lord

Jesus has another aspect. It is not for the cleansing of sin, but it is to give life and to give life abundantly. And that is the reason why when the soldier thrust that spear into His side, out of His heart comes out water and blood—blood to cleanse our sins; water to give us life.

Dear brothers and sisters, when we think of the blood and fat, we believe it is all for ourselves. But remember, the blood and the fat are primarily for God. They are the food of God, God's bread. God feasts upon that. Why? Because the blood satisfies God's righteousness. And the fat satisfies God's holiness. As a matter of fact, the blood and the fat are primarily for God, not for us. It is only secondarily for us.

Oftentimes, we just think of the blood and the fat for ourselves: Christ is for us. We claim the blood upon us. We claim the fat for us. But do we know that Christ is for God? Do we ever present the blood and the fat to God as His bread? Now that is priesthood—a holy priesthood to offer spiritual sacrifices, acceptable to God through Jesus Christ.

Do you not know that we should be a people who worship God in spirit and in truth? And what do we bring to God? We bring to God the Christ that He has given to us. We bring to God the blood. We bring to God the fat. We bring to God the Christ that we know, and as we bring the Christ that we know back to God, remember God feeds upon Christ. This is our worship. This is our ministering unto God. Whenever we come to God, we just thank Him for the blood. We just thank

Him for the fat. We thank Him for Christ Jesus. And as we come to God, and bring Christ back to Him and say, "Oh God, how we appreciate Thy son," the Father is satisfied. He feeds upon that. That is our worship. Do we minister unto the Lord?

Three—Communion with the Lord

> They shall enter into my sanctuary, and they shall approach unto my table, to minister unto me (Ezekiel 44:16a).

In Ezekiel's vision, he only saw the table in the house of God. This is the table of the Lord. And yet, a preceding verse says it is an altar made of wood. In other words, that table is a combination of the golden altar of incense and the golden table of shewbread. These two just joined together, and it is the privilege of the priests to minister unto God by the table. In other words, we come to the table.

A table speaks of communion. When we break bread together, we fellowship with one another. We share Christ together. So, as we approach the table, we commune with God. Oh, brothers and sisters, there is nothing that pleases God more than communion.

As parents, how you love your children to approach you just to be near you—sometimes with looks, sometimes with words, and sometimes even without words, even when they are just sleeping— but they are in your bosom. How satisfying it is to you parents. It is more precious than if your children gave you a bar of gold.

Brothers and sisters, how often we think that God is a hard master. He just wants to work us to death. No, we will work, but He primarily wants our fellowship. Oh, if only we would draw near to the table, just to be with Him. Look up to Him with words, sometimes with no word. That is ministry unto the Lord.

And, of course, that table is also an altar. It is the golden altar of incense. Out of communion with Him, He will show His heart to you, and as He opens up His heart to you, you take up His burden and begin to pray; you offer incense.

In the fifth chapter of the book of Revelation and in its eighth chapter, we find incense is burning. It is the prayers of the saints. The prayers of the saints are like incense to God, of course, mingled with the merits of Christ, in His name. Are we just praying, "God, give us this and give us that; I need this, and I need that"? Our heavenly Father knows what we need.

If we read Revelation chapter five, we find that the prayer of the saints goes up as incense. It is praise. It is worship. Prayer takes the form of praise and worship. Oh, how we need to worship and praise Him. This is the prayer of our hearts. Not to ask Him for anything but to thank Him for what He has done and to praise Him for what He is. Who can do that? The priests.

And if you read Revelation chapter eight, what is the prayer there? You find that God is going to do something upon this earth, but He withholds that until He hears His children asking for it: "Thy will be done on earth as it is in heaven." Then, God begins to work.

Dear brothers and sisters, are we praying such prayers? Such prayer is ministering unto the Lord because it prepares and opens the way for the will of God to be done upon this earth. What a privilege! It is as if God has brought us into the secret counsel and revealed His heart and His burden to us. Then, we stand with Him and say, "Lord, this is what we want because this is what You want." And God says, "All right. I will do it."

Four—Keep the Charge

Ministering unto the Lord is: "…they shall keep my charge" (Ezekiel 44:16b). The Levites who went astray during the falling away of the children of Israel could not keep the charge of the house. They could guard the gates, but they could not keep the charge of God. God only put the charge upon the house of Zadok: "They shall keep My charge." Now, what does it mean? It means that they are to minister unto the Lord to preserve the testimony of God. Only those who are faithful can maintain the testimony of Jesus today. What a privilege!

Instructions to the Priests

Then you will find the instruction to these priests. There are certain things that these priests should be very careful about when they enter into the sanctuary and minister unto the Lord.

I—Linen Dress

First, the priests should wear linen dress; everything is linen from the head to the bottom. They should not wear anything made of wool. Why? Because in ministering unto the Lord, they should never sweat.

Linen comes from plants, taken care of by our heavenly Father. Linen speaks of that which is pure, bright, white, and shiny. In other words, it speaks of the power of God.

When ministering to the Lord, you can only minister in the power of God, the power of the Holy Spirit. You do not need to sweat. But wool comes from animals. If you put wool on, you will sweat, and sweat is the result of the curse.

When Adam and Eve were tending the Garden of Eden, though they would go from one tree to another tree to prune, they would never sweat. But after they were driven out of the Garden of Eden, they had to sweat in order to make a bare living. What a difference!

If you are ministering unto the Lord, you never sweat. There is rest in your spirit. But if you try to do things in your own power, in the power of the flesh, oh, how you will sweat! And sweating is exhausting. When you minister unto the Lord, it is only in the power of the Holy Spirit. You never have to sweat.

II—Trimmed Hair

Secondly, a priest should not shave his head, nor allow his locks to grow long, but he shall have his head polled [hair trimmed]. You know, shaving the head is to expose your head. It is considered to be a shame, and it is a sign of mourning. When people were in mourning, they shaved their heads. That was the custom. But no, a priest should not shave his head; he has to have his head covered. A priest is under the authority of God (see Ezekiel 44:18).

And then, he cannot let his locks grow long. (Long hair is the glory of women.) If you are a Nazarite, you have to have your hair grow long. But remember, this is not a Nazarite, this is a priest. So, a priest should not let the hair grow long—neither shaved nor growing long—but to have his hair polled [trimmed] (see Ezekiel 44:20).

Now, what does that mean? It means that on the one hand, a priest is under the authority of God (having his hair covered, not shaved), but on the other hand, he is to represent God's authority (having his hair trimmed, not long). There is a balance there—neither shaving nor growing long, but trimmed. That is the divine order (cf. I Corinthians 11:1-6). Anyone who ministers as a priest is under the authority of God. If you are not under the authority of God, you have no authority whatsoever. On the one hand, you need to be under the authority of God; on the other hand, you need to be willing to represent God's authority. And this is how you can serve as a priest.

III—No Intoxication

Thirdly, when a priest enters the sanctuary, he should never drink wine. He should never be intoxicated. He should never have his mind confused because he is to separate the clean from the unclean, the holy from the profane.

Do you remember what happened when the two sons of Aaron—Nadab and Abihu—became drunk? They entered the house to burn incense with strange fire. Then, fire came out from the holiest place and burned them to death. And from that day on, God said that no priest can drink wine when he is on active duty (see Numbers 3:4; Leviticus 10:1-4, 8-10; Ezekiel 44:21).

Brothers and sisters, if we want to serve, we have to be separated from the world. If we are not separated from the world, we will be confused. We will not see the difference between clean and unclean, between holy and profane. We will offer strange fire. Our service will not be accepted.

The Reward

Well, we do not have time to go on, but let me say, what is the reward of these priests? The Lord said,

> And it shall be unto them for an inheritance; I am their inheritance: and ye shall give them no possession in Israel; I am their possession. (Ezekiel 44:28).

The Lord is their possession. Whatever the Lord has is theirs. Can there be any reward greater than this?

Oh, that the priesthood may be recovered! That is one thing that needs to be recovered—all God's people functioning as priests. However, even when all God's people function as priests, remember we are not only ministering unto the house, but we must first minister unto the Lord.

The Kingship

And, of course, there is another side, and that is kingship. You will find these chapters mention the prince. (And we know that the prince there signifies Christ.) Why is he called a prince instead of a king? It is because God is King over His people. Though our Lord was born King and yet throughout His life, He acted like a prince rather than a king. In other words, He is a king unto God, not unto himself. He never takes upon himself His own right. He always submitted himself to the Father.

And with the prince, there are princes. Brothers and sisters, we are all princes. We are to rule and reign with Christ. Of course, that speaks of spiritual leadership, spiritual authority. The prince is not the one to lord over the people, but to give the land to the people. Kingship is the ability to subdue the enemy, to bring back the land, and give the land to the children of God. That is the work of the kings. Oh, that we may subdue our enemy, experience the unsearchable riches of Christ, and then give these unsearchable riches of Christ to God's people. That is the work of kings, of princes. May the Lord see the priesthood and the kingship restored. Then the glory of the Lord will rest forever.

Our heavenly Father, may Thy glory fill the house, and may Thou be glorified through the priesthood and the kingship. Forbid that we fail as Thy house, as the priesthood and the kingship. Have mercy upon us that Thou wilt consider us as faithful and Thou wilt commit Thyself to us that we may serve Thee to Thy glory. May God be glorified in the church, in Christ Jesus. Amen.